The People Wish
to See Jesus

POPE FRANCIS RESOURCE LIBRARY

The People Wish to See Jesus

—— Reflections for Those Who Teach ——

JORGE MARIO BERGOGLIO
POPE FRANCIS

Translated by
Michael O'Hearn

In cooperation with

CLARETIAN
PUBLICATIONS

A Herder & Herder Book

The Crossroad Publishing Company
www.CrossroadPublishing.com

English translation copyright 2014
by The Crossroad Publishing Company
A Herder&Herder Book
The Crossroad Publishing Company, New York

The text of *The People Wish to See Jesus* is part of a book
originally published as *El verdadero poder es el servicio.*
Editorial Claretiana, Buenos Aires, Argentina
Chapter titles in the original Spanish publication
have been altered in this English edition.

ISBN 978-08245-2036-6 (alk. paper)

Library of Congress Cataloging-in-Publication Data
available from the Library of Congress.

Cover image: Photograph taken during World Youth Day in Brazil
(Getty Images)

Cover design by George Foster
Book design by The HK Scriptorium, Inc.

In continuation of our 200-year tradition of independent publishing, The Crossroad
Publishing Company proudly offers a variety of books with strong, original voices
and diverse perspectives. The viewpoints expressed in our books are not necessarily
those of The Crossroad Publishing Company, any of its imprints or of its employees.
No claims are made or responsibility assumed for any health or other benefit.

Books published by The Crossroad Publishing Company may be purchased at special quantity discount rates for classes and institutional use. For information, please
e-mail sales@CrossroadPublishing.com.

Printed in the United States of America in 2014.

Contents

Contents

Introductory Note

Editorial Claretiana has been publishing short books by the Archbishop of Buenos Aires for several years, and they have been very well received by the public. The texts are taken from the homilies and workshops Jorge Mario Bergoglio gave as Archbishop of Buenos Aires, and the volumes and chapters have been organized by themes. While some of the text are specifically addressed to the people of Argentina, these writings provide an excellent service to the whole People of God. And with Cardinal Bergoglio having become Pope Francis, these texts offer precious insights into the thoughts and practices that have shaped the first pastor of the Catholic Church.

Part I

To Teachers and Catechists

"The words that I have spoken to you
are spirit and life." (John 6:63)

Catechists, into the Streets!

"REPENT, AND BELIEVE IN THE GOSPEL." This is what the priest said to us last Wednesday during the imposition of the ashes.

We begin Lent with this mandate: Break our heart, open it so that it believes in the Gospel of truth, not in the erudite Gospel or the light Gospel or the watered-down Gospel, but in the Gospel of truth. Today, this Gospel is asking you in a special way, as catechists, "to repent, and believe in the Gospel."

But this also gives you a mission in the Church: to act in such a way that others will believe in the Gospel. Watching you, seeing what you do, how you behave, what you say, how you feel, how you love—this will lead them to the Gospel.

The Gospel says that the Spirit led Jesus into the wilderness, and there he lived among the wild beasts as if nothing would happen. This reminds us of what happened in the beginning: The first man and the first woman lived among the beasts and nothing happened. In this paradise all was peace and joy. And they were tempted, and Jesus was tempted.

Jesus wants to repeat, at the start of his public life, after his baptism, something similar to what happened in the beginning. This gesture of Jesus to live in peace with all of nature, in the fertile solitude of the heart and in temptation, is a sign to us of

Homily to Catechists, Archdiocesan Catechetical Meeting, March 2000.

what he came to do. He came to renew, to recreate. In one of the Mass prayers during the year, we say something very beautiful: "God, how admirably you create all things and more admirably recreate them."

Jesus, in the wonder that was his vocation of obedience, came to recreate, to reconcile things, to bring harmony even in the midst of temptation. Is this clear? And Lent is this path. In Lent we all must make room in our heart so that Jesus, by the power of the Spirit, the same Spirit who led him into the wilderness, may reconcile our heart. But the Spirit does not reconcile it, as some might wish, with special prayers and cheap feelings of intimacy; rather, the Spirit reconciles it with a mission, with apostolic work, with daily prayer, work, effort, and witness. Make room for Jesus because time is running out, says the Gospel. For the last two thousand years we have been in the time that Jesus set in motion, the time of reconciliation.

Time is of the essence. We have no right to be satisfied with coddling our soul and remaining enclosed in our small things . . . tiny things. We have no right to be comfortable, to be in love with ourselves. "How I love myself!" No, we don't have that right. We have to go out and proclaim that, two thousand years ago, there was a man who wanted to restore the earthly paradise, and he came to do it, to reconcile all things. And so we have to proclaim this to "doña Rosa," whom we see on the balcony. We have to proclaim to the young people, to those who have lost hope, to those for whom everything is "insipid," everything is tango music, everything is *cambalache**. We have to proclaim this to the self-satisfied, overweight woman who thinks that by losing weight she will gain eternal life. We have

---

* *Cambalache* is literally a bazaar or junkshop. In Argentina, however, the term refers to a slang-language tango song written in 1934 that criticized twentieth-century corruption.

to proclaim this to all those young people, like the ones we see on the balcony, who claim that everyone wants to put them in the same mold. The tango lyric didn't say, but could have said, "No matter what happens, it is all the same."

We have to go out and talk about him to the people of the city we see on the balconies. We have to leave our shells and tell them that Jesus is alive, that Jesus lives for him, that Jesus lives for her; and we have to say so with joy, even though at times this seems a little bit crazy. The Gospel message is foolishness, says Saint Paul. A lifetime is not long enough to dedicate ourselves to proclaiming that Jesus is restoring life. We must go and sow hope; we must go into the streets. We have to go out and search.

So many old people like that doña Rosa are weary with life and at times do not have enough money to buy medicine. How many ideas do we put into the heads of little children, ideas we collect like great innovations, ideas we think are great educational developments, when ten years ago they were already being thrown into the garbage in Europe and the United States.

So many young people spend their lives spaced out on drugs and noise, because they have no direction, because no one told them that there was something great! So many nostalgic people in the city need a tin countertop in a bar where they keep drinking one grappa after another so they can forget!

And there are so many good people; but being vain and preoccupied with appearances, they run the risk of falling into pride and arrogance.

Are we going to stay home? Are we going to stay locked in the parish? Are we going to stay in the gossip of parish, school, or church structure? When all these people are waiting for us! The people of our city! A city with religious resources, with cultural resources, a precious and beautiful city, but one that is greatly tempted by Satan. We cannot hide, we cannot stay in the parish or the school. Catechists, into the streets! To catechize, seek out, knock on doors, knock on hearts!

The first thing that she (the Virgin Mary) did, when she received the Good News in her womb, was to run out to serve. Let us run out to serve by bringing to others the Good News that we believe in. May this be our conversion: the Good News of Christ yesterday, today, and always. Amen.

The People Wish to See Jesus

EVERY SECOND SATURDAY OF MARCH, we have an opportunity to get together for the Archdiocesan Catechetical Meeting (EAC). There, together, we revisit the annual cycle of catechesis, focusing on a key idea that will take us through the year. This is an intense time of meeting, celebration, and communion that I greatly value, and I am sure that you do too.

Now, as the feast of St. Pius X, the patron of catechists, approaches, I want to address each of you with this letter. In the midst of the activities, when fatigue starts to set in, I wish to encourage you, as a priest and a brother, and invite you to take a break to reflect together on some aspect of catechetical ministry.

I am aware that, as bishop, I am called to be the first catechist of the diocese. But above all I would like to use this meeting to overcome a little of the anonymity of the big city that often impedes the personal encounters that clearly all of us are seeking. In addition, this can be one more means of charting common lines for archdiocesan catechetical ministry that will allow for a basic unity within the logical and healthy plurality typical of a city as large and complex as Buenos Aires.

In this letter, I have decided not to focus on some aspect of catechetical praxis but rather on the person of the catechist.

Many documents remind us that the whole Christian

Homily to Catechists, Archdiocesan Catechetical Meeting, March 2001.

community is responsible for catechesis. This makes sense, since catechesis is an aspect of evangelization. And it is the entire Church that evangelizes; consequently, at this period of teaching and deepening in the mystery of the person of Christ, it should not be the responsibility of catechists or priests only, but of the whole community of the faithful (see *Catechesi tradendae*, 16). Catechesis would be seriously compromised if it were relegated to the isolated and solitary action of catechists. That's why there will be no lack of effort to raise awareness. The path undertaken years ago to achieve an organic pastoral plan has contributed markedly to a greater involvement of the entire Christian community in this responsibility for Christian initiation and mature education in faith. In the context of this co-responsibility of the whole Christian community for the transmission of the faith, I cannot ignore the reality of the person of the catechist.

The Church recognizes in the catechist a form of ministry that, throughout history, has permitted Jesus to be made known from generation to generation. Not in an exclusive form but in a privileged way, the Church recognizes in this part of the People of God a chain of witnesses of whom the *Catechism of the Catholic Church* says, "The believer has received faith from others. . . . Each believer is a link in the great chain of believers. I cannot believe without being carried by the faith of others" (*CCC,* 166).

In recalling our own personal process of faith development, we discover the faces of humble catechists who, with their witness to life and their generous commitment, helped us to know and fall in love with Christ. I remember with affection and gratitude Sr. Dolores from Misericordia de Flores School. She was the one who prepared me for First Communion and Confirmation. And until a few months ago, another of my catechists was still living: it did me good to visit her, welcome her, and phone her. Today, too, there are many young people and adults who silently, humbly, and simply continue being instruments of the Lord to build community and make present the Kingdom.

That is why I am today thinking about each catechist and highlighting an aspect I feel has great urgency in the present circumstances in which we are living: catechists and their personal relationship with the Lord.

With great clarity John Paul II warns us in his apostolic letter *Novo millennio ineunte* (*NMI*): "Ours is a time of continual movement which often leads to restlessness, with the risk of 'doing for the sake of doing.' We must resist this temptation by trying 'to be' before trying 'to do.' In this regard we should recall how Jesus reproved Martha: 'You are anxious and troubled about many things; one thing is needful' (Luke 10:41-42)" (*NMI*, 15).

In the being and vocation of every Christian is the personal encounter with the Lord. To seek God is to seek his face, to enter into his intimacy. Every vocation, especially that of the catechist, presupposes a question: "Master, where do you live?" and an answer: "Come and you will see." From the quality of the answer, from the depth of the encounter, will emerge the quality of our meditation as catechists. The Church is constituted on this "Come and you will see." Personal encounter and intimacy with the Master underpin true discipleship and guarantee the genuine flavor of catechesis, pushing aside the ever-present rationalisms and ideologies that drain away vitality and sterilize the Good News.

Catechesis needs holy catechists whose mere presence is contagious, and whose life witness helps to overcome an individualistic civilization dominated by "a minimalist ethic and a shallow religiosity" (*NMI*, 31). Today, more than ever, we urgently need to let ourselves be found by the Love which always takes the initiative to help us experience the Good News of the encounter.

Today, more than ever, you can see in so many of our people's demands a search for the Absolute, which, at times, takes on the form of an outraged humanity's painful cry: "We wish to see Jesus" (John 12:21). Many are the faces that, with a silence more telling than a thousand words, demand this of us. We know them well: They are in the midst of us; they belong to the faithful people whom God entrusts to us—they are the faces of children, of young people, of adults. Some look like the "beloved disciple," others like the prodigal son. There is no lack of faces marked by pain and despair.

But all are hoping, searching, and wanting to see Jesus. For this reason believers, especially catechists, must "not only 'speak' of Christ, but in a certain sense 'show' him to them. . . . Our witness, however, would be hopelessly inadequate if we ourselves had not first *contemplated his face*" (*NMI*, 16).

Today, more than ever, current difficulties oblige those whom God has called to console his People to be rooted in prayer so they can "confront *the most paradoxical aspect of his mystery*, as it emerges in his last hour, on the Cross" (*NMI*, 25). Only through a personal encounter with the Lord can we provide loving service without breaking down or letting ourselves be overwhelmed by pain and suffering.

Today, more than ever, any movement toward our brothers and sisters, any ecclesial service, must assume and be based on a closeness to, and familiarity with, the Lord. Like Mary's visit to Elizabeth, rich in service and joy, it can only be understood and become a reality through the profound experience of meeting and listening that occurred in the silence of Nazareth.

Our people are tired of words; they don't need teachers so much as they need witnesses.

And witnesses gain inner strength through an encounter with Jesus Christ. All Christians, and catechists even more so, must be permanently disciples of the Master in the art of prayer. "We have to learn to pray: as it were, learning this art ever anew from the lips of the Divine Master himself, like the first disciples: 'Lord, teach us to pray!' (Luke 11:1). Prayer develops that conversation with Christ that makes us his intimate friends: 'Abide in me and I in you' (John 15:4)" (*NMI*, 32).

Hence we must also understand Jesus' invitation to launch out into the deep as a call to pluck up the courage to throw ourselves into the depths of prayer so that the thorns will not choke out the seed. Sometimes our fishing is unsuccessful because we don't do it in his name, because we are too preoccupied with our nets, and we forget to do it with and for him.

These times are not easy; nor are they times for fleeting whims, or for isolated, sentimental, or Gnostic spiritualities. The Catholic Church has a rich spiritual tradition, with many and various teachers who can guide and nourish a true spirituality that today enables the loving service of listening and the ministry of encounter to happen. In a careful and receptive reading of chapter 3 of the pope's letter *Novo millennio ineunte,* you will find the inspirational source of much of what I want to share with you. Simply, to end, I would encourage you to work on three fundamental aspects of the spiritual life that apply to all Christians and especially to catechists.

1. The personal, living encounter through a prayerful reading of the Word of God.

I thank the Lord because his Word is increasingly present in the meetings of catechists. As well, I am certain that the biblical formation of catechists has progressed significantly. But we risk staying in a cold exegesis or use of Sacred Scripture if there is no personal encounter, the irreplaceable reflection that every believer and community must do so that the Word may produce "a life-giving encounter, in the ancient and ever valid tradition of *lectio divina,* which draws from the biblical text the living word which questions, directs, and shapes our lives" (*NMI*, 39). In this way catechists will discover the inspirational source for all their teaching, which will necessarily be marked by the love that becomes presence, offering, and communion.

2. *The personal, living encounter through the Eucharist.*

We all experience the joy, as Church, of the close, daily presence of the risen Lord until the end of history. It is the central mystery of our faith; it creates communion and strengthens us in mission. The *Catechism of the Catholic Church* reminds us that in the Eucharist we encounter all the good of the Church. In her we are certain that God is faithful to his promise and will be with us until the end of time (Matthew 28:20).

In the adoration of the Blessed Sacrament, we experience the nearness of the Good Shepherd, the tenderness of his love, the presence of a faithful friend. We have all experienced the great help provided by faith, that intimate, personal dialogue with our sacramental Lord. And catechists cannot waver in this beautiful vocation to proclaim what they have seen (see 1 John 1).

In the celebration of the breaking of the bread, we are called once again to imitate his handing over of himself and to repeat this unique gesture of multiplying acts of solidarity. From the eucharistic banquet the Church experiences communion and is invited to make efficacious the miracle of "neighbor empathy," which enables us, in this globalized world, to provide a place for our brothers and sisters and to ensure that the poor feel at home in every community (see *NMI*, 50). Catechists are called to make the doctrine the message, and the message, life. This is the only way the proclaimed Word can be celebrated and truly constitute the sacrament of communion.

3. The joyful community encounter of the Sunday celebration.

Easter—the passage of the Lord who entered into history to make us participants in his divine life—is made present in the Sunday Eucharist. We assemble around the altar every Sunday as the family of God, which is nourished by the Living Bread, and which brings and celebrates what happens along the way to renew our strength and to continue proclaiming that he lives among us. In every Sunday Mass we experience our deeply felt belonging to this People of God into whom we were incorporated by Baptism, and we commemorate the "first day of the week" (Mark 16: 2, 9). Today's world, which is often unhealthy because of secularism and consumerism, seems to be losing its ability to celebrate and to live as a family. For this reason catechists are called to commit their lives so that Sunday is not stolen from us and to encourage what is in the human heart to continue the celebration and to find meaning and fullness of its journey throughout the week.

Saint Teresa, with that power of synthesis typical of souls great and simple, wrote to one of her sisters, summarizing what the Christian life consisted of: "to love him and to make him loved." For all catechists, this is your reason for being. Only if you have a personal encounter can you be an instrument for others to encounter him.

Greeting you on this Catechist's Day, I want to thank you with all my heart for your service to our faithful people. And I ask Mary Most Holy to keep alive in your heart this thirst for God so that you will never tire of seeking his face.

Keep praying for me that I may be a good catechist. May Jesus bless you and may the Blessed Virgin take care of you.

Worship Enables Empathy

Perhaps more than at any other time in our history, this scarred society awaits a new coming of the Lord. It awaits the healing, reconciling coming of the one who is the Way, the Truth, and the Life. We have reason to hope. We do not forget that his passage and salvific presence have been a constant in our history. We are discovering the wonderful stamp of his creative work in a nature of incomparable richness. Divine generosity is also reflected in the witness of the life, dedication, and sacrifice of our parents and ancestors, as well as in the millions of humble, believing faces, our brothers [and sisters], anonymous leaders of work and heroic struggle, incarnation of the silent epic of the Spirit who founds peoples.

However, we are far from the gratitude this received gift deserves. What prevents us from seeing the coming of the Lord? What makes it impossible to "taste and see that the Lord is good" (Psalm 34:8) given the generosity of the land and the people? What impedes our nation from seizing the opportunity to fully encounter the Lord and his gifts? As in the Jerusalem of his time, when Jesus was passing through the city and that man Zacchaeus couldn't see Jesus because of the big crowd, something is preventing us from seeing and feeling his presence.

Homily to Catechists, Archdiocesan Catechetical Meeting, August 2002.

I BEGAN MY *Te Deum* homily last May 25 with those words. And I would like them to serve as the introduction to this letter that I am sending you with grateful affection as you go about your silent but important task of building up the Church.

I don't believe I am exaggerating when I say that we are in a time of "spiritual myopia and moral turpitude," which leads us to regard as normal a "shallow culture" in which there seems to be no room for transcendence and hope.

But by being a catechist and from the knowledge you have acquired through your weekly dealings with people, you know well that the desire and need for God continue to pulse in humanity. Given the pride and arrogant self-importance of the new Goliaths who, using new media and government offices, bring to the fore self-absorbed prejudices and ideologies, David's serene trust has become more necessary than ever to defend our heritage. This is why I want to reiterate what I wrote to you last year:

> *Today, more than ever, you can see in so many of our people's demands a search for the Absolute which, at times, takes on the form of an outraged humanity's painful cry: "We wish to see Jesus" (John 12:21). Many are the faces that, with a silence more telling than a thousand words, demand this request of us. We know them well: they are in the midst of us, they belong to the faithful people whom God entrusts to us—they are the faces of children, of young people, of adults. Some look like the "beloved disciple," others like the prodigal son. There is no lack of faces marked by pain and despair.*
>
> *But all are hoping, searching, and wanting to see Jesus. For this reason, believers, especially catechists must, not only "speak" of Christ, but in a certain sense "show" him to them.... Our witness, however, would be hopelessly*

inadequate if we ourselves had not first contemplated his face (*NMI* 16).

That is why I want to propose to you that we pause this year to explore the subject of worship.

Today, more than ever, we need to "worship in spirit and truth" (John 4:24). This is the indispensable task of the catechist who wants to be rooted in God and not waver in the midst of so much turmoil.

Today, more than ever, we need to worship to enable the "neighbor empathy" that these times of crisis demand. Only in contemplating the mystery of Love that overcomes distances and becomes nearness will we find the power to overcome the temptation of passing by, without stopping on the way.

Today, more than ever, we need to teach those being catechized to worship so that our catechesis is truly initiation and not only instruction

Today, more than ever, we need to worship to avoid overwhelming people with words that sometimes obscure the Mystery. We need to give ourselves silence that is full of admiration and that is quiet before the Word that is present and near.

Today, more than ever, worship is necessary!

To worship is to prostrate ourselves, to humbly acknowledge the infinite greatness of God. Only true humility can acknowledge true greatness and recognize something small trying to appear as something great. Perhaps one of the greatest perversions of our time is worshiping what is human and ignoring the divine. "You shall worship the Lord alone" is the great challenge to such empty and vacuous notions. Not to worship contemporary idols—with their siren songs—is the great challenge of the present; not to adore the unadorable is the great sign of our times. Idols that cause death deserve no adoration whatsoever; only the God of life merits "worship and glory" (see *Documents of Puebla,* 491).

To worship is to look with trust at the one who is trustworthy because he is the giver of life, instrument of peace, and creator of encounter and solidarity.

To worship is to stand tall in front of all that is unadorable because worship sets us free and fills us with life.

To worship is not to empty but to fill ourself, to acknowledge and enter into communion with Love. No one adores one who doesn't love; no one adores one they do not consider to be their love. We are lovers! God is love! This certainty is what leads us to worship with all our heart the one who "loved us first" (1 John 4:10).

To worship is to discover his tenderness, to find comfort and rest in his presence, to experience what Psalm 23 describes: "Even though I walk through the darkest valley, I fear no evil; for you are with me. . . . Goodness and mercy shall follow me all the days of my life."

To worship is to be a joyful witness of his victory, to understand great tribulation, and to have a foretaste of the celebration of the encounter with the Lamb, the only one worthy of worship, who will dry all our tears and in whom we celebrate the triumph of life and love over death and abandonment (see Aparecida document, 21–22).

To worship is to draw near to unity, to discover that we are children of the same Father and members of one family and, as Saint Francis discovered, to sing praise together with all creation and all humanity. It is to reestablish the bonds we have broken with the earth and with our brothers and sisters, and to acknowledge him as Lord of all things and loving Father of the whole world.

To worship is to say "God" and to say "life." To encounter

the God of life face to face in our daily life is to worship him with our life and witness. It is to know that we have a faithful God who is with us and who trusts us.

To worship is to say Amen!

Greeting you on this Catechist's Day, I want to thank you again for your service to this faithful People. And I ask Mary Most Holy to keep alive in your heart this thirst for God so that you can, like the Samaritan in the Gospel, "worship in spirit and truth" and "make many draw near to Jesus" (John 4:39).

Keep praying for me that I may be a good catechist. May Jesus bless you and may the Blessed Virgin take care of you.

A Pedagogy of Presence

"**B**UT WE HAVE THIS TREASURE in clay jars, so that it may be made clear that this extraordinary power belongs to God and does not come from us" (2 Corinthians 4:7).

Throughout this year, we are trying, as the archdiocesan Church, to attend to "the fragility of our people," also making this the theme and style of the archdiocesan mission.

In this vein, I would like to include the theme of "fragility" in the letter that I write to you every year on the occasion of the feast of Saint Pius X, the patron of catechists.

In 2002 I invited you to reflect on the mission of the catechist as a worshiper, as one who has learned before a mystery so great and wonderful that it overflows him to become prayer and praise. Today I wish to dwell on this aspect. In the face of a fragmented world, in a country tempted by new fratricidal divisions, in the face of the painful experience of our own fragility, it is necessary and urgent, indispensable I would say, to delve deeper into prayer and worship. It will help us to unify our heart and give us "bowels of compassion" to be persons of encounter and communion, who accept as our own the vocation to take care of our brother's wounds. Do not deprive the Church of its ministry of prayer, which allows you to oxygenate the everyday tiredness that comes from giving witness to a God so near, so Other: Father, Brother, and Spirit; Bread, Companion on the Journey, and Giver of Life.

Letter to Catechists, August 2003.

One year ago I wrote: "Today, more than ever, we need to worship to enable the 'neighbor empathy' that these times of crisis demand. Only in contemplating the mystery of Love that overcomes distances and becomes nearness will we find the power to overcome the temptation of passing by, without stopping on the way."

It was precisely the text of the Good Shepherd (Luke 10:25–37) that shone forth on the *Te Deum* of May 25 of this year. This same text invited us "to give new meaning to our life—as persons and as a nation—from the joy of the risen Christ that allows the hope of living as a true community to spring up, in the very fragility of our flesh."

To proclaim the kerygma, to give new meaning to life, to build community—these are tasks the Church entrusts to catechists in a particular way, great tasks that surpass and at times overwhelm us. In some way we can see our reflection in the young Gideon, who, before being sent to fight against the Midianites, felt helpless and bewildered by the apparent superiority of the invading enemy (Judges 6:11–24). Before this new pseudo-cultural invasion that presents us with the new pagan faces of the "Baals" of long ago, we too experience the disproportion of Gideon's strength and smallness. But it is precisely in the experience of our fragility when strength from above, the presence of the one who is our guardian and our peace, shows itself.

That is why I dare to invite you this year to use the same contemplative eyes with which you discover the nearness of the Lord to recognize in your fragility the hidden treasure that confounds the arrogant and pulls down the mighty. Today the Lord invites us to embrace our fragility as the source of a great evangelizing treasure. To see ourselves as mud, jar, and path is also to render worship to the true God.

Only those who can acknowledge their vulnerability are capable of solidarity action. Thus, to be moved by and to sympathize with a person who has fallen on the side of the road—these are the attitudes of those who know how to recognize in the other their own image, a mixture of dirt and treasure, and for this reason do not reject it. Indeed, they love it, draw near to it and unwittingly discover that the wounds that heal their neighbor are ointment for their own. Compassion turns into communion, into the bridge that draws near and builds relationships. Neither highway robbers nor those who walk past the fallen person are aware of their treasure or their mud. That's why the robbers do not value the life of others and disrespectfully leave them almost dead. If you don't value your own life, how can you recognize as treasure the life of others? Those who walk past, in turn, value their life but only partially, and dare to look only at the part they think has value: they know they are chosen and loved by God (conspicuously in the parable they are two religious persons in Jesus' time: a Levite and a priest) but are afraid to recognize themselves as clay, as fragile mud. That's why the fallen person scares them, and they don't know how to admit it. How will they be able to acknowledge the mud of others if they do not accept their own?

If there is anything that characterizes catechetical pedagogy, if there is anything in which catechists should be experts, it is their capacity to welcome, to take care of the other, to ensure that no one is left by the side of the road. That is why, given the seriousness and extent of the crisis and the challenge to us as archdiocesan Church to commit ourselves to "care for the fragility of our people," I invite you to renew your vocation as catechists and put all your creativity in "knowing how to be" near those who suffer, making of reality a "pedagogy of presence," in which listening and "neighbor empathy" are not just a style but the content of catechesis.

And in this beautiful artisanal vocation of being "chrism and balm for those who suffer," don't be afraid of caring for the fragility of your brothers and sisters out of your own fragility: God will transform your pain, weariness, and brokenness into richness, ointment, and sacrament. Remember what we considered together on the feast of Corpus Christi: there is a fragility, the Eucharist, that hides the secret of sharing. There is a fragmentation that makes it possible, in the loving act of surrendering oneself, to nourish, unify, and give meaning to life. On this feast of Saint Pius X, may you prayerfully present to the Lord your weariness and fatigue, like that of the persons whom the Lord has put on your path, and let the Lord embrace your fragility, your mud, to transform it into an evangelizing power and a source of strength. This is what the apostle Paul experienced: "We are afflicted in every way, but not crushed; perplexed, but not driven to despair; persecuted, but not forsaken; struck down, but not destroyed; always carrying in the body the death of Jesus, so that the life of Jesus may also be made visible in our bodies" (2 Corinthians 4:8–10).

We are called to be catechists in our fragility. Our vocation would not be full if it excluded our mud, our falls, our failures, our daily struggles; in fragility the life of Christ manifests itself and becomes a saving proclamation. And from it the voice of the prophet becomes Good News for all:

Strengthen the weak hands, and make firm the feeble knees. Say to those who are of a fearful heart, "Be strong, do not fear! Here is your God. . . . He will come and save you." Then the eyes of the blind shall be opened, and the ears of the deaf unstopped: then the lame shall leap like the deer, and the tongue of the speechless sing for joy. . . . They shall obtain joy and gladness, and sorrow and sighing shall flee away" (Isaiah 35: 3–6, 10).

May Mary help us to appreciate the treasure of our mud so that with her we may sing the Magnificat of our smallness next to the greatness of God.

Keep praying for me that I may also live this experience of limitation and grace. May Jesus bless you and may the Blessed Virgin take care of you. With all my affection.

Spirituality of the Journey

A S A PILGRIM DIOCESAN CHURCH, we will soon experience a strong moment of the Spirit: the next Assembly of
the People of God. I wish that in this time of preparation we
initiate a journey of prayerful community discernment.

As the Church in Argentina we are pilgrims on our way to
Corrientes, where, in a few more days, we will come together
as a faithful People around the Eucharist to ask the Lord that
its daily celebration will help us realize our dream, so often
delayed, of being a nation truly reconciled and united. We do
this sadly recognizing that there are people who have nothing
to eat in this land blessed with bread.

Identity, memory, membership in a pilgrim people.

In this dynamic reality of the Church, as the feast of Saint
Pius X approaches, I send you my warmest greetings and heart-
felt thanks for Catechist's Day. I want to share with you a few
reflections that have recently been the subject of my prayers,
in line with what I wrote to you on Ash Wednesday, when I
invited you to look after the fragility of your brothers and sisters with the audacity of Jesus' disciples who trusted in his risen
presence.

We know that there is a temptation to remain trapped by
paralyzing fear that sometimes dressed up as withdrawal, and
realistic assessment, and, at other times, as routine repetition.

Letter to Catechists, August 2004.

But the cowardly, conformist urge of a shallow culture, accustomed only to the security of walking by, is always below the surface.

Apostolic audacity implies searching, creativity, and launching out into the deep!

In this spirituality of the journey there is also the great temptation to betray the call to walk as a people, renouncing the mandate of the pilgrimage madly to run the marathon of success. In this way we mortgage our way of life, joining the culture of exclusion in which already there is no place for the elderly or the molested child, and no time to stop at the side of the road. The temptation is great because it is supported by new modern dogmas such as efficiency and pragmatism. That's why much audacity is needed to go against the current and not renounce the possible utopia that is precisely the inclusion that sets the style and rhythm of our step.

Walking as a people is always slower. Furthermore, no one can deny that the journey is long and difficult. Like in that foundational experience of the People of God in the wilderness, there will be no lack of weariness and bewilderment.

All of us, at one time or another, have found ourselves stuck and disoriented on the road, not knowing which way to go. Oftentimes reality leaves us confined, without hope. Like the people of Israel, we doubt the promises and presence of the Lord of history, and we let ourselves be enveloped in the positivist mentality that seeks to provide the interpretive key of reality. We give up our vocation to make history in order to add ourselves to the nostalgic chorus of complaints and reproaches: "Is this not the very thing we told you in Egypt, 'Let us alone and let us serve the Egyptians?' For it would have been better for us to serve the Egyptians than to die in the wilderness" (Exodus 14:12). Apostolic zeal will help us to remember, to not give up our freedom, to walk as people of the covenant: "Take care that you do not forget the Lord, who brought you out of the land of Egypt, out of the house of slavery" (Deuteronomy 6:12). As catechists in difficult times, you must ask God for the audacity and zeal that will help you to remember! "Take care and watch yourselves closely, so as not to forget the things that your eyes have seen" (Deuteronomy 4:9). In the memory passed on and celebrated, we as a people will find the necessary strength to avoid falling into anxiety and paralyzing fear.

This journey of the People of God recognizes times and rhythms, temptations and trials, and graced events in which it becomes necessary to renew the covenant.

Today, too, in our journey as Church in Buenos Aires, we are living a very special moment that encourages us to detect a time of grace. We want to open ourselves to the Spirit who will set us in spiritual movement so that the next diocesan assembly will be a true "time of God" in which, in the presence of the Lord, we can delve deeper into our identity and our awareness of mission, and have an experience of fraternal and communal discernment in which prayer and dialogue allow us to overcome misunderstandings and to grow in community and missionary holiness.

Any journey obliges us to start, to get going; it unplugs us and places us in situations of spiritual combat. We must pay special attention to what is happening in our hearts, and to the movement of various spirits (good, bad, personal) so that we can discover and discern God's will.

We must not be surprised as we start this journey at the appearance of the subtle temptation of the "alternative" seduction; it expresses itself in never accepting a common path and always presenting other possibilities as absolutes. This is not an instance of healthy, enriching pluralism, or differing nuances, at the time of community discernment; rather, it is an inability to walk with others, because in the depths of the heart there is a preference to travel alone along elitist paths that in most cases lead us to fall back egotistically on ourselves. The catechist, however, the true catechist, has the wisdom that develops from being close to the people and to the richness of so many faces and shared histories that distance him or her from any trendy version of "enlightenment."

Do not be surprised that on the way there may be evil spirits who reject anything new, cling to what has been acquired, and prefer the security of Egypt to the promises of the Lord. That evil spirit leads us to revel in difficulties, to bet on the first failure, to say goodbye "with realism" to the multitudes because, deep down, we do not know how, are unable, and do not want to include them. No one is immune to this evil spirit.

Hence, the invitation to renew our zeal is an invitation to ask for God's grace for our Church in Buenos Aires: the grace of apostolic audacity, the strong and zealous audacity of the Spirit.

We know that this spiritual renewal cannot be the result of a movement of the will or a simple change of mood. It is grace, interior renewal, profound transformation that is based and supported in a Presence that, as on that afternoon of the first day of the new history, walks with us to transform our fears into fervor, our sadness into happiness, our flight into proclamation.

You only need to recognize him as at Emmaus. He keeps on breaking bread so that they will recognize us in the breaking of our bread. And if we lack the audacity to take on the challenge of feeding others, let us do in our life what God told the tired, overworked prophet Elijah to do: "Get up and eat, otherwise the journey will be too much for you" (1 Kings 19:7).

In thanking you for your journey as a catechist, I ask our eucharistic Lord to renew your apostolic zeal and fervor so that you never get used to the faces of so many children who do not know Jesus, the faces of young people who wander through life without meaning, the faces of the excluded multitudes who, with their families and old people, struggle to be a community, whose everyday steps through our city hurt and challenge us.

More than ever we need your closer look as a catechist to contemplate, moving and stopping as often as is necessary, so that we can give to our journey the healing rhythm of "neighbor empathy." You can then experience true compassion, the compassion of Jesus, which does not paralyze but rather motivates and impels you to go out with more strength and more audacity to proclaim, cure, and liberate (see Luke 4:16–22).

More than ever we need your sensitive catechist's heart, which brings, from your experience of accompaniment, the wisdom of life and of the processes that nurture prudence, the ability to understand, the art of waiting, the sense of belonging in order to guard the sheep entrusted to us from the erudite wolves that are trying to pull the flock apart.

More than ever we need your person and catechetical ministry so that, by your creative actions, you can, like David, infuse music and joy into the tired steps of our people (2 Samuel 6:14–15).

Please pray for me that I may be a good catechist. May Jesus bless you and may Mary look after you.

Love, Look, Cherish,
Then Teach

"A ND HE APPOINTED TWELVE . . . to be with him, and to
be sent out to proclaim the message" (Mark 3:13–14).
Mark's text allows us to enter into the perspective of the one
called.

Behind every catechist, every one of you, there is a call, a
choosing, a vocation. This is the true foundation of our identity: we have been called by God, chosen by him. We believe
and confess the initiative of love that is at the origin of who we
are. We recognize ourselves as gift, as grace.

And we have been called to be with him. That's why we call
ourselves Christians and acknowledge our close relationship
with Christ. With the apostle Paul we can say, "It is no longer I
who live, but it is Christ who lives in me" (Galatians 3:20). This
living with Christ is truly a new life: the life of the Christian,
and it determines all that we are and do. Thus, all catechists
must aim to abide in the Lord (John 15:4) and prayerfully care
for their hearts transformed by grace because it is what you
have to offer and where your real treasure lies (see Luke 12:34).

Perhaps some of you are thinking to yourself, "But what you
are telling us could be applied to all Christians." Yes, that's true.
And that is exactly what I want to share with you this morning.
Every catechist is first and foremost a Christian.

Homily to Catechists, EAC, March 2005.

This may seem rather obvious. Nonetheless, one of the Church's most serious problems, and one that often endangers its evangelizing efforts, lies in those pastoral agents—those of us who are most interested in the "things of God" and most integrated into the ecclesiastical world—who frequently forget to be good Christians. Then begins the temptation to make absolute and categorize spirituality—the spirituality of the layperson, of the catechist, of the priest—with the grave risk of losing its Gospel originality and simplicity. And once the common Christian horizon is lost, we give in to the temptation of the snob, of the affected, of the person who entertains and puts on weight but who neither nourishes nor helps others to grow. The parts become the distinctive features, and in favoring the parts we easily forget the whole, the very people we are forming. Then the centrifugal movements begin; they are not at all missionary but quite the contrary: they scatter us, distract us, and, paradoxically, they entangle us in internal and fragmented pastoral concerns. Let us not forget that the whole is greater than the part.

I think it important to insist on this because a subtle temptation of the Evil One is to make us forget our common belonging that has its source in Baptism. And when we lose our identity as children, brothers and sisters, and members of the People of God, we occupy ourselves cultivating an artificial, elitist pseudo-spirituality. We stop crossing the fresh green pastures and remain entrapped in the paralyzing sophisms of a "test-tube Christianity." Now we are no longer Christians but "enlightened elites" with Christian ideas.

Bearing this in mind, we can now point out specific features.

Catechists are men and women of the Word—with a capital W. "But he went out and began to proclaim it freely, and to spread the word. . . . People came to him from every quarter"

(Mark 1:45). "Many heard him and were astonished" (Mark 6:2). "They were all amazed, and they kept asking one another, 'What is this? A new teaching—with authority!'" (Mark 1:27). "And he appointed twelve, whom he also named apostles, to be with him, and to proclaim the message" (Mark 3:14). "And they went out and proclaimed the good news everywhere" (Mark 16:20).

This relationship of the catechist to the Word has more to do with "being" than "doing." There can be no authentic catechesis without the centrality of, and reference to, the Word of God, which animates our actions, sustains them, and makes them fruitful. Catechists commit themselves before the community to meditate and reflect on the Word of God so that their words will be an echo of it. Thus, they receive it with the joy inspired by the Spirit (1 Thessalonians 1:6), interiorize it, and ponder it like Mary (Luke 2:19). In the Word they discover wisdom from on high that will permit them to do the penetrating discernment that is necessary at both the individual and the community levels.

"Indeed, the word of God is living and active, sharper than any two-edged sword, piercing until it divides soul from spirit, joints from marrow; it is able to judge the thoughts and intentions of the heart" (Hebrews 4:12).

Catechists are servants of the Word; they let themselves be educated by it, and in it they have the serene trust of a fruitfulness that exceeds their own strength: "My word . . . shall not return to me empty, but it shall accomplish that which I purpose" (Isaiah 55:10–11). Catechists should take to heart what John Paul II says about the priest: "The priest ought to be the first 'believer' in the word, while being fully aware that the words of his ministry are not 'his,' but those of the one who sent him. He is not the master of the word, but its servant" (*Pastores dabo vobis,* 26).

So that this listening to the Word is possible, catechists must be men and women who like silence. Yes! Because catechists are men and women of the Word, they should also be men and women of silence—contemplative silence that allows them to rise above the word inflation that reduces and impoverishes their ministry to a hollow wordiness, like so much of what contemporary society offers us. Dialogic silence makes respectful listening to the other possible and thus enhances the Church with the loving service of the Word that offers itself as the response. Silence filled with "neighbor empathy" complements the Word with decisive action that facilitates the encounter and makes possible the "theophany of us." That is why I dare to invite you, as men and women of the Word, to love silence, to seek silence, and to make silence fruitful in your ministry!

But if anything special should characterize catechists, it is their look. Catechists, says the *General Directory for Catechesis*, are experts in the art of communication. "The summit and center of catechetical formation lies in an aptitude and ability to communicate the Gospel message" (no. 235). Catechists are called to be teachers of communication. They want and seek to make the message become life, and without disregarding the contributions of present-day communication sciences. In Jesus we always have the model, the way, the life. Like the Good Teacher, every catechist should show the "loving look" that is the beginning and condition of any truly human encounter. The Gospel accounts spare no verses to document the profound mark that Jesus' look left on the first disciples. Never tire of looking with the eyes of God!

In a civilization paradoxically wounded by anonymity and at the same time unashamedly sick with unhealthy curiosity about the other, the Church needs the close look of the catechist to contemplate, move, and stop as often as necessary to give our journey the healthy rhythm of "neighbor empathy." In this world it is precisely the catechist who should make present the fragrance of the gaze of Jesus' heart. Catechists will have to initiate their brothers and sisters in this "art of accompaniment" so that children and adults learn always to remove their sandals before the holy ground of the other (see Exodus 3:5). This respectful, healthy look, filled with compassion, is essential given the gloomy spectacle of the media's manipulative omnipotence, and the arrogant, disrespectful gurus of monolithic thinking, found even in government offices, who want us to give up our defense of human dignity, contaminating us with an inability to love.

For this reason I ask you as catechists to take care of your look! Do not surrender your dignifying look. Never close your eyes to the face of a child who does not know Jesus. Don't divert your look, don't become distracted. God has placed you and sent you so that you may love, look, cherish, and teach. And the faces that God entrusts to you are not to be found only in the parish hall or in the church. Go farther: be open to the new crossroads in which fidelity takes on the name creativity. You will surely remember that the *General Directory for Catechesis* proposes the parable of the sower to us. Bearing in mind this biblical horizon, don't lose the identity of your look as catechists. For there are many ways of looking. Some look for statistics, and all they see are numbers, all they can do is count. Others look for results, and all they see are failures. Still others look with impatience, and all they see are long waits.

Let us ask the one who got us into this planting to look with the eyes of the good sower who is brimming over with tenderness, to share in his look: a look that is trusting and long-term; a look that does not give in to the sterile temptation of wanting to check on what was sown every day, because it knows that whether asleep or awake the seed will grow on its own; a hopeful, loving look that, when separating the wheat from the chaff, does not react in a complaining or alarmist way, because it knows and remembers the free fruitfulness of charity.

But if anything is typical of catechists, it is their recognition of themselves as men and women who proclaim. Clearly, all Christians should participate in the Church's prophetic mission, but catechists should do so in a special way.

What does it mean to proclaim? It is more than saying or telling something. It is more than teaching something. To proclaim is to affirm, shout, communicate; it is to share with all your life. It is to bring to the other your own act of faith, which, to be all-encompassing, becomes action, word, visit, communion. And we are not proclaiming a cold message or a simple body of doctrine. First and foremost we are proclaiming a Person, an event: Christ loves us and has given up his life for us (see Ephesians 2:1–9). Catechists, like all Christians, proclaim and testify to a conviction: that Christ has risen and is living among us (see Acts 10:34–44). Catechists offer their time, their hearts, their gifts, and their creativity so that this conviction may become life in others, and so that God's plan may become history in others. It is also proper to catechists that their proclamation, which centers on a person, Christ, should also announce his message, his teachings, and his doctrine. Catechesis is teaching. That has to be said straightforwardly. Don't forget that as catechists you are engaged in the Church's missionary activity. Without a systematic presentation of the Faith, our following of the Lord will be incomplete, it will be difficult to explain what we believe, and we will be complicit in large numbers of people not reaching maturity in the faith. And even though at some moments in Church history kerygma and catechesis were too separate, today they should be united, though not identified, with each other. In this time of unbelief and widespread indifference, catechesis should have a strong kerygmatic dimension. But it can't be only kerygmatic or it will cease to be catechetical in the long run. It must shout out and proclaim that "Jesus is Lord!" but it must also lead the catechumens gradually and pedagogically to know and love God, to enter into his intimacy, and to initiate them into the sacraments and the life of the disciple.

Never stop proclaiming that Jesus is Lord. Help precisely to make him truly "Lord" of those being catechized. Help them to pray in depth, to enter into his mystery, to taste his presence. Do not water down the content of catechesis or reduce it to simplistic ideas, which, when they leave their human setting, their rooting in the person, in the People of God and the history of the Church, lead to sickness. Ideas understood in this way end up as words that say nothing and can transform us into modern-day nominalists, into "enlightened elites."

In this context, witness becomes very important. Catechesis, as faith education, as the transmission of dogma, always demands the support of witness. This holds for all Christians, but for catechists it takes on a special dimension: catechists are called and sent by the Church to give witness. Witnesses are the ones who have seen something, and they want to talk about it, describe it, and communicate it. In catechists, a personal encounter with the Lord gives not only authenticity to their words but also credibility to their ministry, to what they are and to what they do.

If catechists have not contemplated the face of the Word made flesh, they don't deserve to be called catechists. Moreover, they may end up being labeled imposters because they are deceiving those being catechized.

And another thing: you are catechists in this time, in this

impressive city of Buenos Aires, in the diocesan Church that is journeying together. That is why catechists in this time of crisis and change should not be ashamed to state their convictions. Not everything is changing, not everything is unstable, not everything is the fruit of culture or consensus. There is something that has been given to us as a gift that exceeds our abilities, that goes beyond anything we can think or imagine. Catechists must experience in their own ministry what the evangelist John describes: "So we have known and believe the love that God has for us" (1 John 4:16). We are certainly facing a difficult time of much change, and this has us talking about a change of epoch. Catechists in this new and challenging cultural context will occasionally feel troubled and perplexed but never despondent. Remembering the action of God in our lives, we can say with the apostle, "I know the one in whom I have put my trust" (2 Timothy 1:12). At this time of historic crossroads and great crisis, the Church needs the fortitude and perseverance of catechists who, with their humble but certain faith, are helping new generations to say with the psalmist: "By my God I can leap over the wall" (Psalm 18:29). "Even though I walk in the darkest valley, I fear no evil: for you are with me" (Psalm 23:4).

You work as catechists in Buenos Aires, a city of considerable size and complexity, makes what you do rather unique. You are *porteño* catechists!* This means that the particularities of this great city will distinguish you from catechists in any other place.

Every large city has many resources, many possibilities, but also many dangers. One of these is exclusion. Sometimes I wonder if, as a diocesan Church, we are complicit in this culture of exclusion in which already there is no place for the elderly or the molested child and no time to stop by the side of the

---

* *Porteño* refers to a resident of Buenos Aires.

road. The temptation is great because it is supported by new modern dogmas such as efficiency and pragmatism. That's why much audacity is needed to go against the current in order not to abandon the possible utopia that is precisely the inclusion that characterizes the style and pace of our journey.

Be daring and think of pastoral work and catechesis from the perspective of the periphery, from those most on the margins, those who are absent from the parish. They too are invited to the marriage of the Lamb. For several years now I have been saying to the EAC, "Get out of your caves!" Today I say it again: "Get out of the sacristy, out of the parish office, out of the VIP halls! Get out! Do your pastoral work in the public squares, at the doors, in the houses, on the streets. Don't wait! Get out!" And above all provide a catechesis that does not exclude, that is attuned to different rhythms, that is open to new challenges in this complex world. Don't become rigid bureaucrats, fundamentalist planners who exclude.

God has called you to be their catechists. In this Church of Buenos Aires that is passing through the Spirit times, be active leaders in the diocesan assembly, not by controlling or imposing, but rather by sharing with others in the exciting experience of discernment and of letting God be the author of history.

Each year you come together as catechists at EAC. EAC is synonymous with communion. For one day you leave behind your work in the parish to experience the richness of communion, the beautiful symphony of the distinct and the common. It is a day of sharing, of enriching yourself with others, of experiencing living in the courtyard of La Salle, the "meeting tent," where week after week you proclaim Jesus to adults and children. You are also experiencing this communion with other pastoral agents, with other members of the faithful. They may be deacons, that is, servants virtually obsessed with communion. Join yourselves to this breath of the Spirit that invites us to overcome our *porteño* individualism that canonizes the expression "stay out." For a little while, get rid of that nostalgic, tango-like, it-won't-work mentality to defeat the old, tired prophets of gloom we meet along the way.

In today's world there is much pain and many sad faces from whom the paschal joy of the Good News of the Gospel that we believe in is hidden. For this reason, proclaim that Jesus is Lord with joy—the profound joy that has its origin in the Lord.

With catechists of the whole country we ask God for this grace during the ENCA (National Meeting of Catechists of Argentina). That is why you will march together with the catechists of Greater Buenos Aires on April 24 to guard and preserve the ability to celebrate, the joy of traveling with the other, and the joy of knowing you are brothers and sisters in the beautiful vocation of catechist. You will travel lightly, with a heart full of fervor. And you will do this in Luján*, together with our faithful Mother, so that she will help you to encounter her Son, and in him, all the People of God who are journeying in the land of Argentina.

You will renew your vocation; you will confirm your mission. You will ask for the grace to be instruments of communion, so that in making the Church a home for all, you can make God's tenderness present in life's painful situations, even in those moments of conflict that I know can be glimpsed in the not-too-distant future.

May Mary of Luján grant us what we ask with the catechists of the entire country: "May our ministry be one of listening, proclamation and joy."

---

* Luján is a city located sixty-eight kilometers from Buenos Aires. It is best known for its large neo-gothic basilica, built in honor of the Virgin of Luján, the patroness of Argentina.

Teach with Authority

THE FEAST OF SAINT PIUS X and the celebration of Catechist's Day is a suitable occasion to tell you how grateful I feel for your quiet, committed dedication to the ministry of catechist.

Ministry, directed at so many children, young people, and adults, is one of the ways that the Church today realizes the Lord's command: "Go into the world and proclaim the good news to the whole creation" (Mark 16:15).

Ministry of the Word that has much to do with proclamation, teaching, faith education, discipleship, and Christian initiation.

Ministry of the servant Church that wants to make present and close the One Master, who has the "words of eternal life" (John 6:67).

Ministry that needs us to be prayerful (Luke 22:46) and happy to be with him (Mark 3:14), so that, from the ever-renewing and liberating experience of encountering the Messiah, you may be more witness than teacher, because the proclamation is simplified and takes on the power of Good News when at the center of catechesis and the Church's whole life there is a person and an event: Christ, his Easter, his love.

Only thus can the ministry have authority, offering in these times of such disintegration the invaluable service of making present and near the Good Teacher who teaches with authority.

Letter to Catechists, August 2006.

This is clearly not the authority that the world envisions, which is closer to eloquence, power, or fancy titles, but the authority that produced astonishment and admiration among the ordinary people who were Jesus' contemporaries. This is about authority and wisdom that have nothing to do with learning that is puffed up and self-absorbed, but rather, in the etymological sense of authority, as "that which nurtures and augments" (from the Latin *autoritas, de augere*). You are called, as catechists, to accompany, to lead to the tranquil waters so that the encounter becomes source, celebration, and shelter.

That is why I demand that you listen, and teach others to listen, just as Jesus did. And not simply as an attitude to facilitate an encounter between persons, but fundamentally as an essential element of the revealed message. Indeed, throughout the whole Bible the same invitation recurs: Listen!

For this reason it will be a part of your ministry not only to know how to listen and to help others listen but mainly to show God that you know how and want to listen.

It was exactly this idea that we all prayed about a few days ago on the feast of Saint Cajetan.

The reading from Exodus tells us something very simple and, at the same time, very beautiful and consoling: God listens to us; God, our Father, listens to the cry of his people, the silent cry of the interminable line of people who pass by [the statue] of Saint Cajetan. Our heavenly Father hears the rumble of our steps, the prayer that murmurs in our hearts as we approach.

Our Father listens to the sentiments that move us, remembering our loved ones, seeing the faith of others and their needs, recalling things both beautiful and sad that happened to us this year. God listens to us.

He is not like the idols that have ears but do not listen. He is not like the powerful who listen to what suits them. He listens to everything, including the complaints and anger of his children. And not only does he listen, but he loves to listen. He loves to be attentive, to hear well, to hear everything that happens to us. . . .

There is no need to be surprised that on this road we are traveling as the diocesan Church in recent years the theme of listening has come up on more than one occasion.

Because learning to listen will permit us to take the first steps so that the warm welcome that is so desired will become a reality in our communities. Those who listen in a healthy way can transform personal ties, which were so often hurtful, with the simple balm of acknowledging that the other is important and has something to say to me. Listening fosters dialogue and makes possible the miracle of empathy that overcomes distance and resentments.

This attitude frees us from certain dangers that can undermine our pastoral style: the danger of fencing ourselves in as Church, building walls that prevent us from seeing the horizon; the danger of being a self-referential Church that lurks in the crossroads of history and is capable of gutting the best pastoral initiatives; the danger of impoverishing catechesis by conceiving of it as mere instruction or simple indoctrination with concepts that are old and distant in time.

The listening attitude will help us not to betray the freshness and energy of the kerygmatic proclamation by turning it into a concocted, watered-down posturing that, even more than "the Way,"* becomes sludge that blinds and entangles

---

* A divisive U.S.-based fundamentalist sect active in Argentina.

people. We have to train ourselves to listen so that our evangelizing action takes root in that interior sphere that shapes the authentic catechist, who, beyond his activities, knows how to make his ministry a loving service of accompaniment.

Listening is more than hearing. Hearing is related to information. But the first thing about real communication is the heart's ability to make nearness possible; without this there can be no authentic encounter. Listening helps us to find the timely gesture and word that draw us out of the always more comfortable condition of spectator.

As a catechist, do you want to promote true catechetical encounters? Ask the Lord for the grace to listen! The Lord has called you to be a catechist, not simply a communications technician. God has chosen you to make present the warmth of Mother Church, the indispensable womb, so that Jesus may be loved and known today.

To listen is also the ability to question and search together, to journey together, and to move away from any superiority complex so that we unite in the common task that becomes pilgrimage, belonging, people.

It's not always easy to listen. Sometimes it's more convenient to become deaf by adjusting our headphones so we cannot hear anymore. We can easily substitute listening with emails, messages, and "chats," and thereby abstain from listening to the reality of faces, looks, and hugs. We can also preselect who we listen to and listen only to those who, logically enough, interest us. In Church circles there is no lack of flatters to tell us exactly what we want to hear.

To listen is to care for, understand, value, respect, and save what others say. We need the means to listen well, so that all may speak and so that what each person wants to say is taken into account. There is something of martyrdom in listening, something of dying to oneself that recreates the sacred action of the Exodus: Remove your sandals, walk carefully, do not trample. Be quiet, this is holy ground. Does anyone have something to say! Knowing how to listen is a very great grace! It is a gift you need to ask for and train in.

It has always caught my attention that when Jesus is asked what is the greatest commandment, he answers with the famous Jewish prayer called the *Shema*. In Hebrew the word means "listen," and it is the name of one of the most important texts of Sacred Scripture:

> Hear, O Israel, the Lord is our God, the Lord alone.
> You shall love the Lord your God with all your heart,
> and with all your soul, and with all your might.
> Keep these words I am commanding you today in your
>   heart.
> Recite them to your children and talk about them
> when you are away,
> when you lie down, and when you rise.
> Bind them as a sign on your hand
> and fix them as an emblem on your forehead.
>   (Deuteronomy 6:4–9)

For the people of Israel this prayer is so important that pious Jews kept it on small rolls fastened to their forehead or to the arm close to the heart. It constitutes the first and principal teaching, and it is transmitted from father to sons, and from generation to generation. Behind all this is the conviction, communicated from one generation to the next, that the only way to learn and transmit God's covenant is by doing this: listening.

Jesus adds to this first commandment another that follows in importance: "The second is this: 'You shall love your neighbor as yourself.' There is no other commandment greater than these" (Mark 3:31).

Listen in order to love; listen in order to enter into dialogue and respond. On other occasions he says, "Listen to the Word of God and put it into practice" so that he can speak about the call of, and the response to, God's love. Listening to and being touched by those who suffer is his permanent attitude. There is no possibility of love of God and neighbor without this first attitude: listening to them.

In this same line, Saint Benedict introduced his monastic rule that has so influenced the life of the Church: "Listen carefully, my child, to your Master's precepts, and incline the ear of your heart" *(Prologue of the Rule of St. Benedict).*

Saint Benedict summarizes for us, in this first piece of advice, the whole of monastic wisdom. The original verb that he uses in Latin is *obsculta*, which in addition to "listen" means to "sound out," "examine," "explore," "observe," and "recognize." This is to listen by inclining the ear to our heart in such a manner that in all it examines and in all it observes, it knows how to open itself to everything the Master wants to say so that it can enter into communion with him.

Bearing in mind these things, at this time when we recognize ourselves as Church in assembly, I invite you to take on, as part of the ministry the Church has entrusted to you, the pedagogy of dialogue. Thus you will make present, with your gestures and timely words, the face of Mother Church, marked by an authentically dialogic attitude.

To dialogue is to be attentive to the Word of God and to let ourselves be asked questions by him; to dialogue is to proclaim his Good News and also to know how to sound out the questions, the doubts, the sufferings and hopes of our brothers and sisters whom we accompany and acknowledge as our companions and guides on the journey.

This will be a very valuable service to the Church and a concrete way to get out and meet the men and women of Buenos Aires who, regardless of their religion, as human beings, crave and seek spaces of genuine dialogue.

Listen in order to make true dialogue possible today! At all levels and in all areas. Dialogue, encounter, respect: these are the constants of God, trinitarian and near, who has made you a participant in his pedagogy of salvation. Never forget: as a catechist, more than speaking you must listen; you are called to dialogue.

Mary is the expert in all this. Like no one else, her life consisted of listening to God and looking to the needs of others. May she teach us to have the attentive eyes of the heart so we can be today, in this long-suffering, heathen Buenos Aires, disciples of Jesus and brothers and sisters to all.

> *The Lord God has given me the tongue of a teacher, that I may know how to sustain the weary with a word. Morning by morning he wakens—wakens my ear to listen to those who are taught. The Lord God has opened my ear, and I was not rebellious, I did not turn backward (Isaiah 50:4–5).*

Please pray for me that I may be a good catechist. May Jesus bless you, and may the Blessed Virgin look after you.

Model of the Tireless Pilgrim

THE CHRISTIAN LIFE IS ALWAYS a journey in the presence of God, but it is not exempt from struggles and trials, such as we hear in the first reading, in which there appears an old man known to all of us: Abraham. Abraham is the figure of the faithful believer, model of the tireless pilgrim, the man with a healthy fear of the Lord to the point of not denying God his own son, the man who will be blessed with many descendants.

Today Abraham questions us, the Church in Buenos Aires in assembly, about the way in which we are walking in God's presence. There are many ways to walk in the presence of God. Abraham's way was authentic, irreproachable, in liberty, and without fear because he trusted the Lord. God was his strength and his shield, as the psalm tells us. There is another way, one that we sometimes use, in which we call ourselves pilgrims but when in fact we have chosen the way, pace, and time; we are not disciples, because we are following ourselves, and we are not brothers, because we are doing our own thing. One way or another, we have perhaps already learned the art of making others believe, and even making ourselves believe at times, that this is God's will.

Thus, the Lenten wilderness is always good; it allows us year after year "to go on an interior pilgrimage toward the source of mercy" (Benedict XVI) to purify the heart and to throw light

---

Homily to Catechists, EAC, March 2007.

on the temptations of our journey as Church, and, in your case, the temptations of your journey as catechists. And this is what has brought you together year after year in this place which is the EAC: in an atmosphere of communion and celebration, to raise your eyes to our faithful God so that memory becomes identity, mission, and fraternity.

This is our life as Christians: to look at God and to reflect him in ourselves—a faithful but unsettling and demanding God, who asks for obedience in faith; Christians who admit to being pilgrims, who experience in their lives the jealous step of the God of the covenant but who know how, at the same time, to walk in the loving presence of the Father, to surrender to him with the same intimate trust as did Saint Teresa or Brother Charles de Foucauld. In the life of every Christian, of every disciple, of every catechist, there cannot be lacking the experience of the wilderness, of interior purification, of the dark night, and of obedience in faith, which our father Abraham lived. But here, too, lies the root of discipleship, of abandonment, of the people's experience, which allows us to recognize ourselves as brothers and sisters.

In his providence, you too have experienced being unplugged today on a small scale, and you have left behind the wide patios of La Salle to live the newness that comes with a change of venue. And perhaps I am mistaken, but I think the middle class is suffering from nostalgia, does not enjoy the present, and longs for yesterday's comforts.

That is one thing, but much worse can happen in our spiritual and ecclesial life. If there is one thing that paralyzes life it is to abandon the journey to cling to possessions, security, and business as usual. For that reason the Lord upsets you. And He does it without anesthesia, like He did today to Abraham when He asked Abraham to hand over his son, his dreams, his plans.

God is doing this to him without explanation, initiating him into the school of detachment so that he can be truly free, completely available for God's plans, with a view to making him in this way a collaborator in the great history of salvation for him and, above all, for the people entrusted to him.

Abraham's only words to God, which appear in the text that we have heard today, are: "Here I am." Two times. And these are the only words that Abraham says: "Here I am." And these words, "Here I am," say it all! Like the prophet, like the believer, like the pilgrim, the "Here I am," the "Let it be with me according to your word," the "Amen"—these are the only possible responses. If they are not these, all the rest is noise, distraction, confusion. . . . If we cannot say "Here I am" with our lives, it is better to be quiet and not talk, so that we do not add our voices to the shallow chatter going around in our great city.

What does it cost us to say "Here I am"? Often we put conditions on it.

"Here I am," if it agrees with what I think . . .

"Here I am," if I like the proposal and the time . . .

"Here I am," if it does not mean the end of my plans, projects, hobbies . . .

That's why, on this second Sunday of Lent, a time of interior conversion, I invite you to embody in your lives the interior journey that the status of assembly presupposes: to put ourselves into "spiritual movement" that will allow us to keep incorporating pastoral criteria and appropriate common actions to make present a common manner of being Church today in Buenos Aires.

But none of this is possible if we are installed, shielded, in our little world. When we lose the ability to be open to the newness of the Spirit, we cannot respond to the signs of the times. We cannot be authentic disciples, much less brothers and sisters to all. We are transformed into "everyday Pharisees" who go about closing down our capacity for listening and welcoming and so make our church communities sterile, sad, and old, full of paralyzing fears that often lead us to betray the message and to say and do just about anything, except proclaim the Good News. And when we are not open to the newness of the Spirit, which always has the freshness of communion, we run the risk of living with a certain niggling dislike in our hearts for any opinion held by our brothers and sisters that we do not understand or control.

Let us pay attention to the Gospel for today. The text of Mark says that Peter was so terrified that he didn't know what to say. In Peter, fearful and closed to the Spirit, was born the temptation to remain installed on the mountain, giving up the call to be yeast in the dough. This is the subtle temptation of the evil spirit. It is not tempting him with something coarse, but rather with something apparently pious, but which diverts him from his mission, from that for which he was chosen by God. The look is diminished, and the temptation to stay put also becomes present in the apostle's life. Being well, certain, comfortable, even spiritually controlled can become a temptation on the journey of our life and ministry as catechists. Staying here in our tents, on our mountains, on our seashores, in our parishes, in our beautiful, tidy communities can be, in many instances, not a sign of piety and ecclesial belonging but rather of cowardice, comfort, lack of vision, or routine. And the principal cause is not listening attentively to the Son loved by the Father, not contemplating him, not understanding him.

In his providence the good Lord is allowing us to end this catechist's meeting with the Gospel account of the Transfiguration, which invites us to raise our eyes to the Lord, only to him, so that we can also say, "Here I am." And we can also do this as the Church of Buenos Aires in assembly that asks for the grace "to strengthen the bonds of fraternal charity so that we can create anew the awareness of belonging to the one People of God." To do this we must ask for the grace of a sincere conversion for one another: personal and ecclesial conversion to renew ourselves in the spirit of communion and participation that allows us to overcome our paralyzing fear of walking in the freedom of the Spirit; personal and ecclesial conversion to face the purifications and corrections that allow us to grow in fidelity and to encounter new paths of evangelization; personal and ecclesial conversion to embody in expressions of closeness the pedagogy of holiness, which becomes listening, dialogue, and discernment; personal and ecclesial conversion so as not to be led by the prophets of "it doesn't work," so as not to be left ill with a disillusioned heart that, as it becomes hardened, loses the beat of celebration and life and embraces only criticisms and fears.

In the midst of this Lenten pilgrimage, may we be able to rediscover the transfigured Christ so that he, and he alone, with his close and loving presence, cures, heals, and overcomes all fear and trembling, because he is God with us—Emmanuel. "If God is for us, who is against us?" (Romans 8:31).

Begin Again from Christ

A s in previous years the feast of Saint Pius X is an occasion for us to give thanks to God together for this beautiful ecclesial ministry in which the Word of God becomes comprehensible and significant in the lives of children, young people, and adults. I do this in the context of our ongoing journey as a diocesan Church in assembly, with a view to discovering the proper attitudes that make possible an evangelization oriented toward the margins so that all, not just some, may have fullness of life.

I am writing to you aware of the enormous difficulties of your task. The transmission of the faith has never been a simple job, but, in these times of epic changes, the challenge is even greater.

> *Our cultural traditions are no longer handed on from one generation to the next with the same ease as in the past. That even affects that deepest core of each culture, constituted by religious experience, which is now likewise difficult to hand on through education and the beauty of cultural expressions. It even reaches into the family itself, which, as a place of dialogue and intergenerational solidarity, had been one of the most important vehicles for handing on the faith* (Aparecida document, 39).

Letter to Catechists, August 2007.

Hence, we must "start over from Christ, from contemplation of him who has revealed to us in his mystery the complete fulfillment of the human vocation and its meaning" (Aparecida, 41). Only be gazing at the Lord can we accomplish our mission and adopt his attitudes.

One of the most enlightening contributions of the recent Aparecida Assembly has been its raising our awareness that maybe the biggest danger to the Church is not to be sought outside but rather within its own children, in the eternal temptation to remain defensive and closed so as to be protected and safe:

The Church cannot retreat in response to those who see only confusion, dangers, and threats, or those who seek to cloak the variety and complexity of situations with a mantle of worn-out ideological slogans, or irresponsible attacks. What is required is confirming, renewing, and revitalizing the newness of the Gospel rooted in our history, out of a personal and community encounter with Jesus Christ that raises up disciples and missionaries. That depends not so much on grand programs and structures, but rather on new men and women who incarnate that tradition and newness, as disciples of Jesus Christ and missionaries of his Kingdom, protagonists of new life for a Latin America that seeks to be rediscovered with the light and power of the Spirit.

A Catholic faith reduced to mere baggage, to a collection of rules and prohibitions, to fragmented devotional practices, to selective and partial adherence to the truths of the faith, to occasional participation in some sacraments, to the repetition of doctrinal principles, to bland or nervous moralizing, that does not convert the life of the baptized would not withstand the trials of time. Our greatest danger is the gray pragmatism of the daily life of the Church in which every-thing apparently continues normally, but in reality the faith is being consumed and falling into meanness. We must all start again from Christ, recognizing that being Christian is not the result of an ethical choice or a lofty idea, but the encounter with an event, a person, which gives life a new horizon and a decisive direction (Aparecida, 11–12).

This centering in Christ, paradoxically, makes us decentralize, because where there is true life in Christ there is also departure in the name of Christ. This is truly to start again in Christ. It is to recognize ourselves called by him to be with him, to be his disciples but in order to experience the grace of the sending, to leave to proclaim, to go to encounter the other (see Mark 3:14). To start again from Christ is to look at the Good Master who invites us to leave our usual path to turn what happens beside the road, at the margin, at the periphery, into the experience of "neighbor empathy" and an authentic encounter with the love that makes us free and whole.

I remember something I shared with you in one of the first EACs many years ago: "One thing that must be borne in mind to give direction to catechesis is that what has been received must be proclaimed" (see 1 Corinthians 15:3). The heart of the catechist is subject to a double movement, centripetal and centrifugal (receiving and giving). Centripetal in that it "receives" the kerygma as gift and welcomes it into the center of the heart. Centrifugal in that the kerygma is proclaimed with existential need ("Woe is me if I do not evangelize"). The gift of kerygma is missionizing: in this tension the catechist's heart is moved. What is required is an ecclesial heart that "listens with reverence to the Word of God and proclaims it with courage" (*Dei verbum* 1).

Permit me to insist on this with you: by being catechists, by accompanying the process of faith development, by being committed to teaching, the "tempter" can make you believe that your sphere of activity is reduced to the intraecclesial and lead you to spend too much time hanging around the church and the courtyard. This often happens. When our words, our horizons, adopt the perspective of a small, closed-in world, we shouldn't be astonished that our catechesis loses the power of kerygma and is transformed into an uninspiring teaching of doctrine, a frustrating transmission of moral norms or an exhausting experience of sowing uselessly.

Thus, "to start again from Christ" is concretely to imitate the Good Teacher, the one who has the Word of Eternal Life and goes out a thousand and one times in search of the person in his most diverse circumstances.

To start again from Christ is to raise our eyes to the Good Teacher: he who knew how to differentiate himself from the rabbis of his time because his teaching and his ministry did not remain localized in the Temple courtyard; he who was able to "make his own path" because he went out to encounter the life of his people so he could make them participants in the first-fruits of the Kingdom (see Luke 9:57–62).

To start again from Christ is to take care to pray in the middle of an aggressively pagan culture lest the soul shrink, the heart lose its warmth, and action become overwhelmed by timidity.

To start again from Christ is to feel seized by his word, by his sending, and not to give in to the minimalist temptation to be content with only conserving the faith, to be satisfied that a few keep coming for catechesis.

To start again from Christ means continually going on pilgrimage to the periphery, like Abraham, the model of the tireless pilgrim, in complete freedom, without fear, because he trusted in the Lord. God was his strength and his shield, so he refused to be stopped on his journey because he was making it in God's presence (see Genesis 17:1).

Furthermore, in the life of every Christian, of every disciple, of every catechist, there cannot be lacking the experience of the wilderness, of interior purification, of the dark night, and of obedience in faith, which our father Abraham lived. But herein lies the root of discipleship. The fatigue of the journey cannot discourage or stop our steps because this would be equivalent to paralyzing life. To start again from Christ is to allow ourselves to be uprooted so as not to cling to possessions, security, and business as usual. And because my soul will rest only in God, I set off for the encounter with souls.

To start again from Christ supposes not being afraid of the periphery. Let us learn from Jonah, whom we have seen on more than one occasion this year. His figure is paradigmatic in these times of change and uncertainty. He is a pious man who leads a tranquil, ordered life. However, because this type of spirituality can bring such order and clarity to the way of living religion, it sometimes leads to rigidly framing the places of mission, to being tempted by the security of "it has always been done that way." And to the frightened Jonah, the sending to Nineveh brought crisis, bewilderment, and fear. What resulted was an invitation to delve into the unknown, into what has no answer, into the periphery of his ecclesial world. And that's why the disciple wanted to escape from the mission, he preferred to flee. . . .

Flight is not good. It often hides betrayal and giving up. It often has a sad face and bitter conversation (see Luke 24:17-18). In the life of every Christian, every disciple, and every catechesis there must be a decision for the periphery, a shedding of one's ways; otherwise, we cannot be witnesses of the Teacher; it will surely be changed into a stumbling block and scandal for others (see Matthew 16:23).

To start again from Christ is to experience at all times that he is our only shepherd, our sole center. That's why to center ourselves in Christ means "to go out with Christ." And, thus, by going out to the periphery we will not distance ourselves from the center, but rather remain on the vine and, in this way, bear true fruit in his love (John 15:4). The Christian paradox demands that the itinerary of the disciple's heart is to leave in order to stay, to change in order to be faithful.

Thus, since that historic blessed Sunday morning, the words of the angel that accompany the announcement of the Resurrection ring out in space and time: "Go, tell his disciples and Peter that he is going ahead of you to Galilee; there you will see him" (Mark 16:7). The Teacher always precedes us; he goes ahead (Luke 19:28), and that is why he sends us on our way, teaches us not to remain quiet. There is nothing more opposed to the Easter event than saying, "We are here, let them come." True disciples know and cherish the command that gives identity, meaning, and beauty to their belief: "Go . . ." (Matthew 28:19). Then the announcement becomes kerygma; religion, full life; and the disciple, a true Christian.

Nevertheless, the temptation to confinement and paralyzing fear also accompanied the first steps of Jesus' followers: "The doors of the house where the disciples had met were locked for fear . . ." (John 20:19–20). Today, like yesterday, we can be afraid. Today, we often keep our doors locked. Let us acknowledge that we are in debt.

Today, in thanking you for your devotion, dear catechists, I am emboldened to ask you once again: go out, leave the cave, open the doors, dare to travel new roads. Fidelity is not repetition. Buenos Aires needs you to continue asking the Lord for creativity and audacity to pass through walls and schemes and make it possible, like the exploits of Paul and Barnabas, to bring great joy to many brothers and sisters (see Acts 15:3).

I invite you once again to raise your eyes and your prayers to the Virgin of Luján. Let us ask her to transform our vacillating, fearful hearts so that, like Saint Paul, we make a reality of a faithful Church, one that knows wounds, dangers, and hardships by discovering that, when love is on our side, nothing can stop the Good News of Jesus from ringing out in the periphery (see 2 Corinthians 11:26).

Please pray for me that I may be a good catechist. May Jesus bless you and may the Blessed Virgin look after you.

PART II

On Education

"My teaching is not mine
but his who sent me." (John 7:16)

Educating in the Context of Culture

AT HARVARD, THE FRONTISPIECE of one of the buildings reads: "Who is man that you are mindful of him?" A magnificent question to be addressed by anyone who wants to enter the field of education. Like us today.

What is expressed there, with so much admiration—the words are taken from Psalm 8—does not stress that God, the psalmist's questioner, is the one interested in his creature. ". . . that you are mindful of him?" The emphasis in put on the "that" of the question. It is the quality of the attention that God gives to human beings that surprises the psalmist. The sum of this attention is brought together in one word in Scripture: love.

And after the surprise, after the impact that the actions of the Creator have on his favorite work, there is another question. The ontological question is posed, the question about the being who benefits from such delights.

What is man? What men are we?

The biblical phrase taken in its context helps us to see two approaches, not antagonistic, to the mystery of the human being: the theological approach, or the route of going back from the works to the nucleus from which they sprouted: the way of philosophy, culture, and science.

The first path brings us, in admiration of the sacred author, to the divine pedagogy for humanity, where his Word leads us

---

Lecture, Christian Association of Businesspeople, September 1999.

to such density of nearness and presence in the midst of history that it becomes one of us: Jesus Christ. Christ fully reveals man to man himself and shows him his dignity.

The question fits because man must know what he is, somehow or other, so that he can go on learning to be what he is. This is given as his essence, as nature, but it must be finished, must go on being realized. And this is the process of humanization that we call education.

The man, along with other men, exercises his potential, and at the same time that he is achieving self-realization, he is creating culture. In culture, the subject is a community, a people, in which a lifestyle is assumed. Education involves a process of transmitting culture.

Humankind is defined by its works, but I should add that we are also that which we aspire to be. For that reason we can be defined as much by our aspirations as by our achievements.

At the end of the millennium there is talk of a cultural crisis, of a crisis of values. And all this touches on the nucleus of the human, as a person, as a society.

What is happening concerns us. We should not forget that evil bursts in and installs itself only when there is not what there should be. Discernment is thus in order.

Cultural Discernment

In this globalized culture, the ruins of what someone has termed "shipwrecked culture" arrive on our shores: the elements of modernity that are tossed aside and of its posterity that keeps gaining ground.

Let us try to recognize and characterize some of its features:

Secular messianism: it appears in different forms that are symptomatic of the social or political focus. Sometimes what is required is a shift of the ethos of the acts of the persons toward the structures in such a way that it will not be the ethos that shapes the structures but the structures that produce the ethos. Hence the road of socio-political salvation prefers to go through the "analysis of structures" and the political-economic actions that result from them. Beneath this lies the conviction that the ethos is fragile while the structures are solid and secure. This touches on the action–structure tension. The ethos does not support the right tension between action and structure (the active is considered to be that which comes from the interiority of the person). Consequently, the ethos is shifted toward the structures, and so they are naturally more stable and more weighty. In losing the sense of purpose (the good of persons, God), the strength of numbers, which the structure possesses, remains.

Relativism: the fruit of uncertainty infected by mediocrity, it is the contemporary tendency to discredit values or, at the least, it proposes an imminent moralism that postpones the transcendent, replacing it with false promises or short-term ends. The disconnection from Christian roots converts values into mere platitudes or simply names.

Relativism is the possibility of fantasizing about reality, thinking of it as if it could be dominated by an order carried out in a game. This leads to valuing and judging solely by subjective impression: it does not depend on practical, concrete, objective norms.

There is a reduction of the ethical and the political to the physical. Good and bad do not exist in themselves; there is only a calculation of advantages and disadvantages. The consequence of displacing moral reasoning is that law can no longer refer to a fundamental image of justice, but becomes the mirror of dominant ideas.

This subjectivist withdrawal from values leads us to "progress through situational consensus." Here we are entering into debasement: "leveling toward the bottom" by means of negotiated consensus. Agreements keep on being made. In the end, the logic of force triumphs.

On the other hand, the reign of opinion begins. There are no certainties or convictions. Everything has value; but from here to "nothing has value" is but a short step.

The contemporary human person is experiencing uprooting and abandonment. He was brought to this point by his excessive enthusiasm for autonomy inherited from modernism. He has lost his support in something that transcends him.

A new nihilism that "universalizes" all things, by annulling and invalidating particularities or affirming them with wholesale violence, brings about their destruction. Fratricidal battles; total internationalization of money and the media; lack of concern for concrete socio-political involvement, and a real participation in culture and values.

We delude ourselves with an autonomous, undistinguished individuality and end up as a number in marketing statistics, an incentive for advertising.

The modern one-sided concept of reason: only quantitative reason (geometry as perfect science), the reason of calculation and experimentation, is entitled to call itself "reason."

The technological mentality and the search for a secular messianism are two expressive features of the contemporary human being, whom we can describe as "Gnostic man": possessor of knowledge but lacking unity, and, on the other hand, needing what is esoteric, in this case secularized, or profane. In this sense it could be said that the temptation of education is to be Gnostic and esoteric, unable to manage the power of technique from the interior unity that produces real ends and the means to attain them on a human scale. And this crisis cannot be resolved by any type of "return" (which a moribund modernity stubbornly tried); rather, it is overcome by means of internal overflow, that is, in the very core of the crisis, assuming it entirely, without remaining in it, but transcending it inwardly.

False hermeneutic that creates suspicion. Deceit is used, which is a lie that fascinates with an apparently unobjectionable structure. Its pernicious effects are manifested slowly.

Or caricaturing truth or what is noble, humorously or cruelly exaggerating one perspective and leaving many others in the dark. This is a way of diminishing what is good. It makes it easy to laugh a thousand and one times, in public or in private, at some value—honesty, nonviolence, modesty—but this leads to a diminishing of this value's desirability and a preference for the installation of its antivalue and the defilement of life.

Or a slogan is used that, with verbal and visual embellishment, takes concepts that are the most valuable and rich, makes one aspect absolute, and deforms the whole.

Ultimately, postmodernity does not bring an aversion to the religious; however, it does force it into the private sphere. A diluted deism results, which tends to reduce faith and religion to the sphere of the "spiritualistic" and the subjective (from which arises a faith without piety). From other corners, fundamentalist positions emerge, and then reveal their impotence and superficiality.

This miserable transcendence, which neither attains nor takes into consideration the limits of immanence, simply reveals why it is incapable of reaching any human limits or touching any wounds.

Closely linked to this paradigm of deism is the process of the hollowing out words (words without proper weight, words that do not become flesh). They are emptied of their content;

hence, Christ does not enter as a Person but as an idea. There is an inflation of words. It is a nominalist culture. The word has lost weight; it is empty. It lacks backbone; it lacks the "spark" that makes it alive and is just silence.

Culture of Encounter

Allow me to make a proposal: we need to create a culture of encounter.

In the culture of the fragment, as some have called it, or of non-integration, it is demanded of us even more in difficult times that we not favor those who try to capitalize on resentment, the neglect of our shared history, or who get immense enjoyment in weakening bonds.

With incarnated realism, never let the suffering, defenseless, anguished faces fail to stimulate and commit us to investigate, study, work and create more! The man, the woman—they should be the heart of our mission.

The man of flesh and blood, with concrete historical and cultural belonging, and the complexity of the human with its tensions and limitations are not respected or taken into account. But it is the human being who should be at the center of our concerns and reflections. The human reality of the limitation of law and concrete, objective norms, the always necessary and always imperfect authority, the compromise with reality—these are insurmountable difficulties for the mentality described earlier.

Let us escape from virtual realities and, as well, the cult of appearances.

It is not possible to educate disconnected from memory. Memory is, in fact, unitive and integrating potential. As understanding left to its own forces breaks down, memory becomes the vital core of a family or a people. A family with no memory hardly deserves the name. A family that does not respect and attend to its grandparents, who are its memory, is a broken family; but a family and a people who remember are a family and a people with a future.

The key is in not inhibiting the creative force of our own history, of our remembered history. The educational sphere, in permanent search of wisdom, is a space set aside for this exercise: to rediscover the principles that permitted the realization of this desire, to rediscover the mission hidden there that struggles to continue unfolding itself.

We see so much unhealthy memory, withdrawn, torn in remembrances incapable of going beyond initial obvious facts, entertained by trendy flashes and currents, passing fancies, and know-it-all opinions that hide the disarray. All these fragments obscure and negate history.

The change in the juridical status of our city doesn't mean "a clean slate." For those who have no past, nothing has been accomplished. Everything is the future, and you have to start from scratch.

From the cultural shelters to the transcendence that is foundational. It is necessary to seek out an anthropology that leaves aside any path of "return" conceived—more or less consciously—as a cultural refuge. Man tends by inertia to reconstruct what existed in the past. This trait is a consequence of the foregoing. Modernity, upon losing its objective support points, turns to the "classical" (but in the sense of the classical world, the ancient world, and not in the sense that we are giving the term) as an expression of what culture should be. On finding itself divided, divorced from itself, it confuses the nostalgia proper to the call of transcendence with the longing for immanent mediations that are equally uprooted. A culture without roots and unity cannot be sustained.

Inclusive universalism through respect for differences. We have to enter into the culture of globalization from the perspective of universality. Instead of being atoms that only acquire meaning in the whole, we need to integrate ourselves in a new, vital, higher-order organic structure that takes in what is ours but does not nullify it. We are incorporated harmoniously, without giving up what is ours, into something that transcends us.

And this cannot happen through consensus, which is a leveling-down, but through dialogue, the comparing of ideas, and the exercise of authority.

The exercise of constructive dialogue is the most human way of communicating. In all areas, space for serious, constructive, and not merely formal dialogue should be established. Exchange that breaks down prejudices and, on the basis of a common search, builds up sharing, but that seeks the interaction of wills to promote common work and shared projects.

Furthermore, at this time when it is said that we are "children of information and orphans of communication," dialogue requires patience, clarity, and a good disposition toward the other. This does not exclude the confrontation of various points of view, but with ideas serving as light rather than as weapons. Let us not compromise our ideas, utopias, possessions, and rights; let us give up only the pretension that they are unique and absolute.

The exercise of authority. Guidance is always necessary, but this means participating in the formality that gives cohesion to the body, not for its own sake but to be totally of service. What impoverishment to the dignity of social coexistence results from the politics of fait accompli, which impedes legitimate participation and promotes the formalities over reality!

Respect for our worldviews that inform from within the contents of the most varied areas of knowledge, from the beginner level to teacher training, is the obligation of those who govern, because it creates respect for legitimate pluralism and for the freedom to teach and learn.

So that the force of life and connectedness we carry within ourselves can be manifested, we, especially those who hold a high degree of political or economic power or whatever type of influence, must renounce our interests or unfair demands that try to go beyond the common good that unites us. We need to take on, with an austere disposition and with greatness, the mission that is now given to us.

The practice of opening up spaces of encounter. Behind the front lines of superficiality and short-sighted opportunism (flowers that bear no fruit) there is a people with collective memory who do not give up walking with the nobility that characterizes them. Community effort and strength, the growth of neighborhood initiatives, the rise of so many self-help movements are signs of the presence of God in the whirlwind of participation without particularisms seldom seen in the country. Our people, who know how to organize themselves spontaneously and naturally, active players in these new social ties, are asking for a place of consultation, control, and creative participation in the areas of social life for which they are responsible. We leaders must be part of the vitality of these new ties. Promoting and protecting them may become our principal mission.

How can we not think of the school as a privileged space for exchange!

Openness to committed personal and social religious experience. Religion is a creative force within the life and history of humankind, and a driving force in every life that is open to religious experience.

How can it be that, in some educational spheres, all the themes and questions are dealt with, except for one that is banned, the great outcast: God?

In the name of a neutrality recognized as impossible, they silence and amputate a dimension that, far from being pernicious, can help immensely in the formation of hearts and social harmony in society.

It is not by suppressing differences in legitimate options of conscience or the open treatment of things related to an individual worldview that we will succeed in inculcating respect for each person and the acknowledgement of diversity as the way to unity.

It would appear that the public space has to be "light," very fluid, and sheltered from any conviction, and that the only stance allowed will be vague, frivolous, or favorable to the interests of the powerful.

Educate . . . and After? . . . Educate

Against this background of problems inside and outside the family, economic issues, violence, and alienation, we must ask ourselves: How can we educate? At the same time we must also ask, How can we not educate? How can we not continue to put our trust in education?

The school makes no sense without a teacher, without a teaching staff. Nor does it make sense if the human being is not put at the center. This happens when structures, curriculum, programs, content, evaluation, and ways of managing are fighting to command center stage.

Postmodern culture presents a model of the person strongly associated with the image of youth. Those who try to look young and who receive treatments to make wrinkles of age disappear are beautiful. The model of beauty is young, informal, casual. Our adult model is adolescent.

Teenagers are thought to possess new ways of feeling, thinking, and acting. But at the same time they are deprived of critical ways to interpret their world and of hope for the future. For these teens, schooling is irrelevant and meaningless. They place no value on what the schools present as necessary to live in this society.

The most experienced teachers, confident in their successful ways of teaching, at times find the world of the teenager to be dark and distant. That is to say, we find ourselves with a young person who has little use for academic knowledge and a teacher who does not acknowledge the questions of adolescents. This is a non-encounter.

There are also young people who are invited insistently to search for pleasure and the source of satisfaction of their desires immediately and painlessly, and who are immersed in the culture of the image as their most natural habitat. The knowledge presented by the school seems quite unattractive, and the teens consider it to be unimportant: it does not emphasize sensory satisfaction, nor does it act as a tool for social mobility or simply for access to employment.

In the school, young people are not finding what they are looking for. We could say with some confidence that the modern school is receiving postmodern students, but that's not all.

The need for consistency is imperative. Accusing one

another will get us nowhere. As a society we must show clarity to overcome misunderstandings and not to waste energies building up on the one hand and tearing down on the other.

What to teach? The very variety and multitude of things that are knowable is immeasurable; how do we bring order to this multiplicity of what to teach and what to learn? Starting only from the material to learn about, there is no authentic ordering perspective. The object of knowledge does not necessarily indicate a goal and a perspective. The ordering perspective must be found in man and in human encounter because education must serve formation, that is, the structuring of life. This perspective, even with all the necessary connectedness to the thing itself, must be at the same time a journey of encounter in which the one who teaches and the one who learns understand each other better in relation to their time, their history, the society, the culture, and the world.

Education should help us to avoid the risk of diminishing ourselves by merely distributing knowledge. Education is not just a matter of selecting concrete offerings of content and methods, but also interpreting and evaluating.

Teacher and student need to arrive at an understanding that cements their common desire for truth: not only to feel connected to things but also uprightness in the way of understanding existence.

What is needed is an education in which the fundamentals remain, and which remains foundational.

Truth, beauty, and goodness exist. The absolute exists. It can, or rather, it should be known and perceived.

What is needed is an education that promotes the weaving of a civil society (that is, civic and civilized). Let education be a place of encounter and communal endeavor where we learn to be society, and where society learns to be a supportive society. We have to learn new ways to build the human city.

Not Just Words: Life

As students, alumni, or parents, all of you know of the growing need of education. Also, as business leaders, surely you have been connected to the world of the school by your involvement in designated internships and education projects in community action. Today, your concern for education is evident in the invitation you extended to me, and I am confidently daring to ask for your continuing efforts to accompany the development of a project of the Archdiocesan Department of Parochial Schools of structurally weak or weakened neighborhoods, aimed at the neediest sectors, through the construction of community centers that address diversity, poverty, the family, and education.

The Church has been present in education, here in Río de la Plata, for some four hundred years. The school of the Society of Jesus was the first one in these parts, and, we would like to say, always present. The Church longs to be able to offer education totally free in the areas of our city where academic failure and problems are most acute, such as Lugano, Doldati, La Boca, and Barracas. We are already working in these areas, but we want to increase our presence and accompaniment, offering the support, training, and follow-up that these children and their families need.

Dear educators, the smallest ones in our society expect a great deal from you and us. I know about the effort and the work that is being accomplished. I also know about the enthusiasm and the ability that can be deployed in this crucial hour for the future of education in our city.

A people who wants to get rid of the poverty of emptiness

and despair; a people with memory that cannot be reduced to a mere entry in a book: therein lies the greatness of our people. I notice in our Argentinean people a strong awareness of their dignity. It is an awareness that has been shaped with significant milestones. Our people have soul, and because we talk of the soul of a people, we can talk of a hermeneutic, of a way of perceiving reality, of a consciousness. Today, in the midst of conflicts, this people can teach us that we need not pay attention to those who try to distill reality into ideas, that we are not served by intellectuals without talent or ethicists without goodness; rather, we have to appeal to the depth of our dignity as a people, to our wisdom, to our cultural reserves. This is a true revolution, not against a system but within: a revolution of memory and affection, memory of foundational, heroic deeds, and memory of the simple gestures that we grew up with in the family. To be proud of our mission is to care for these embers of the heart, to guard them from the deceitful ashes of being forgotten and the conceit of believing that our native land, our city, and our family have no history or that it began with us. Embers of memory that condense, like the heat of a fire, the values that make us great; the way of celebrating and defending life, of accepting death, of tending to the fragility of our poor brothers and sisters, of opening both hands in solidarity before pain and poverty, of celebrating and praying; the dream of working together and, from our common poverty, of molding solidarity.

We are all invited to build the culture of encounter; to make and share this new leaven that is at once the revivifying memory of our best history of supportive sacrifice, of the battle against various slaveries, and of social integration; to convince ourselves once again that the whole is superior to the part, time is superior to space, reality is superior to the idea, and unity is superior to conflict.

Finally, we often ask ourselves with some concern, What world are we leaving to our children? Perhaps it would be better to ask: What children are we giving the world?

The Educational Process

L OOKING AT THE EDUCATIONAL PROCESS we find a few certainties that today are worth taking up, and some challenges that we need to know better to deal with them appropriately. On the other hand too, the art of educating participates in the certainties and challenges of the culture in which it is situated. I will limit my comments to the certainties and challenges and suggest mature ways to address the problem.

Educational Encounter and Mutual Acceptance

The first certainty: to have an educational process you need at least two persons. Education is a spiritual–personal process. In other words, I am talking about an educational encounter. I prefer to define the educator as a person of encounter, and this in two dimensions: he who "draws out something from within" and, being a person of authority, in the etymological sense of the word, "he who nourishes and makes grow" (*autoritas, de augere*).

Even though, in later times, authority was identified with power, it was not like that in the beginning. That is why, in our definition of education, the educator—a leader and a person of authority—is the one who leads to true nourishment, the one who leads along the path of interiority to the font that nour-

Course for Principals, February 2006.

ishes, inspires, makes grow, consolidates, and missions. There are two dimensions of the encounter or, rather, two encounters: the encounter with one's own interiority and the encounter with the educator–authority who leads me along the path to this interior encounter. I call this the educational encounter.

We are talking about educational encounter, and while it suggests companionship, one chooses to educate and the other to be educated. One knows the way and has travelled it many times; the other, trusting in this learning and wisdom, lets himself be led. However, this cannot be reduced to an active–passive equation. Educators also receive from their students, and this reception refines and purifies them. Educational encounter requires mutual acceptance. There is no other way to achieve cooperation that combines the strengths of one another in pursuit of high educational goals than this mutual acceptance.

Overcoming Divisions

Such an encounter helps to overcome the frequent situation of "two warring factions," not always noticeable but present. Let us take into account that any passionate human encounter is also conflictual because of the need for self-denial and the renouncing of selfishness.

This encounter is threatened nowadays simply because the actors (parents, students, teachers, directors, unions, the national state) are not developing a single, common goal; thus, as usually happens in this sad country of ours, the fragmentation and stubborn retention of their own goals by the actors mentioned are serious obstacles to this basic unity that the educational process requires and in which all its splendor and efficiency are to be found.

At the present time, education is suffering from constant

erosion. Any search for unity and encounter is neutralized by interests that, in most cases, are alien to education itself. It has become very problematic to achieve the unity of various actors and the complementarity of opposites. The most common solutions are either the absorption of one of the realities of opposition by the other, or the synthesis of both by some type of Hegelian pact-like accord. However, the most difficult and only constructive thing to do is to overcome conflict on a higher level where virtual realities remain in conflict. In this sense we can say that the strength and vitality of any kind of learning are sustained in non-pact-like accords, characterized by a basic attitude of mutual trust—accords that are exercised by schools, teachers, students, parents, the national state, and the unions, in order to form the citizens our country needs for the future; accords that involve an earlier encounter with dialogic and reconciled opponents, with an eye to the common good.

Actors or Spectators

The erosion, which I referred to above and which was provoked by the interplay of interests alien to education, also has another effect: we have become spectators and ceased to be protagonists of our personal history and our life. We express lots of opinions but we seldom take the lead. We look at and judge everything "from the outside." By saying "from the outside" I am expressing an extremely subjective position. This type of judgment, by not letting go of my subjectivity, is arbitrary; it is usually very hard on others and too easy on itself. This is but one step away from an unjust, and at times anarchic, way of proceeding. None of us actors mentioned above is free of this attitude.

Going in the opposite direction from the path of encounter in its two senses, we are isolated and thus spectators and not protagonists of our own personal history. We live our lives looking at and judging ourselves in line with a paradigm that has more to do with an image we seek or desire than with what we truly are. Fascinated by psychological issues or tangled in them, we don't succeed in glimpsing wider horizons that in some way "oblige" us to get outside ourselves and reach the other in an encounter that is the cement for personal identity and becomes even more necessary for the configuration of the country. This "coming out of oneself" is the indispensable condition for a successful encounter.

The Neighbor Is Waiting for Us

Bridging divisions and taking a leading role: two approaches toward encounter. How does this happen? "To go out of yourself and go to your neighbor" is a vital necessity that is only possible in the context of a fraternal, affective bond; the opposite occurs in a compulsive way, in a hyperactivity of the personality that brings no benefit to the protagonist of education or for those who are with him. For example: the hyperactive go about creating artificially, now by intermittent addictions, now by exaggerating the reasons for justice and turning them into injustice, or by the well-known systematic recourse to grievances or legal claims. That is to say, a climate is created whose pole of attraction is the fragmentation of mobilized force by narrow interests. And then there is the contradiction of resorting to artificial means to achieve the encounter in peace. True and lasting interior peace, the fullness that is wanted and sought, has no other secret than the giving up of one's life so that others may live: love. Fraternal love. Encounter in the context of fraternal love. How would one contrast this love with artificial means?

It is not a question of the *eros* of the Greeks, which more than any other notion communicates romance; and, although it tends to focus on the carnal, *eros* does not always refer to the sensual but rather also includes the desire for unity with the person loved and for exclusive possession.

Nor is it *agape,* that totally self-sacrificing love that can give without expecting anything in return, and which is very descriptive of the disinterested love of God and Christian charity.

I am speaking here of *phileo*, which we know by the adjective "filial" or "fraternal," the love that holds the loved one dear but which always awaits a response. It is a love of relationship, participation, communication, and friendship. Filial–fraternal love creates friends who enjoy closeness and companionship. They share interests and may or may not share time. Obviously, two persons are needed for the fullness of filial–fraternal love, since a response is required on the part of the other to continue having it. It has to do with being best friends with each other. This is the challenge that makes the context of encounter necessary for education.

This Is Not Only a Question of Technique

Within the framework of teaching, the possibility of not devoting oneself to the encounter and of being a spectator rather than an actor is easy to perceive when too much trust is put in technique and the application of technique.

Teachers are not technicians; they have something of the parent in them. If we are talking only of technicians, we are not talking about an educational encounter or a culture of encounter. We are not talking of two or more persons united by indelible bonds but of persons who are related to or know each other through happenstance or supplementary, mechanical means such as techniques.

The most obvious consequence of this perception in the educational field is that it works on the person who should become successful and less with the one who remains behind. Thus, we meet enormous intellects that know a lot, but stunted hearts that feel little (or feel for some). Personal encounters do not develop between two persons when there is no give and take—when one only gives and the other only receives.

An encounter clearly happens, but it is largely peripheral and external. The persons remain involved only externally, mediated by techniques and results, not by enduring, affective ties.

The Backbone in the Hands of Parents

From the vantage point of parents (or those who occupy their place) we recognize that they have lost the leading role in the education of their children and have become spectators, largely by not supporting their children, whether through doubt, lack of knowledge, or some other reason. Here, too, we can speak of a shift of authority toward a "superficial dialoguism" that ultimately avoids encounter.

Interior formation, that of the heart, the innermost dimension of children and youth, has changed hands. It is no longer in the hands of parents but of professionals. If there is a learning problem, it is referred to the psychologist. And then, after the causes are identified, the problem is often remedied by referrals to new professionals who are not teachers. I do not deny or discount professional help. I am simply mentioning this change of hand in harmonious interior guidance.

It used to be said that parents handed off their authority

when they brought their children to the school. They left them in the hands of the teacher and even told him not to be stingy with "a steak" if it was needed. Can you imagine something like that today? Already at home that act of authority transference was being reinforced and was so much like what was happening at the school, often with little possibility of handling the contents that the teacher was using in the classroom.

The parents, or whoever takes their place today, with more opportunities to have a say in what goes on in the classroom, have allowed the backbone of formation to slip away. It is not in their hands but in those of others who are outside of the family and, definitely, of personal reality. Not having encountered parental authority, there is no transparency to authority, and the hearts of the children become (I depoliticize the word) etymologically anarchic.

Reestablishing Ties

Perhaps, for the reasons given, I feel that by undermining the educational journey through the indiscriminate application of models that are imported or merely technical, we have broken the links with the educational encounter, the legacy of the Argentinean school (and a source of pride for decades). And, by breaking the main bond, linking the teacher to the student interiorly, we have lost affective binding with the country, the homeland, and our brothers and sisters. I invite you to reclaim it. For this educational encounter to happen we teachers need more than techniques, we need affection. Trust in your affection. Love what you do and love your students.

From this fraternal, or parental, affection that shapes wisdom, you will form in your students a heart: one that loves their country and their land, without yet knowing it with their eyes;

that admires their heroes because they illumine a path that is difficult but not impossible to travel; that knows and loves its customs and folklore; that is grateful for what it is and what it has, and is not afraid to keep moving and progressing toward those much bigger horizons that challenge it.

Education and Human Dignity

"**I** WISH YOU WERE EITHER COLD OR HOT. So, because you are lukewarm . . . I am about to spit you out of my mouth" (Revelation 3:16). This lack of enthusiasm occasionally disguises itself as mediocrity, narrow indifference, or as that attitude of "stay out" or "I didn't go" that has caused so much harm among us.

Half-measures do not facilitate human encounter and coexistence. We are a people. We are with others and because of others; and, thus, we are for others. Because we are for others, with others, and because of others, we are a people and nothing less than a people.

We are men and women with a capacity for the infinite, with a critical conscience, with a hunger for justice and fraternity. With the desire to know so as not to be manipulated, with a taste for celebration, friendship, and beauty. We are a people who walk, sing, and praise. We are a wounded people and a people with arms wide open, who walk with hope, with "staying power" in bad times and occasionally, a little too quickly, spend wastefully. We are a people with a vocation to greatness.

A God Profoundly Involved with Humanity

Again, as the school term is about to begin, we get together to share about what animates us in our work and, even more, about what constitutes the core of our Christian identity and

---

Message to the Educational Communities, 2006.

the ultimate horizon of our existence: our faith in the risen Christ. This Jesus, whom we confess as Christ, gave and called for definitions. He took sides: he chose the weakest; he did not negotiate the truth; he did not conform. He lived in peace, he defended peace; but he didn't step back when they hit him, the ones who felt his presence to be a nuisance because the people would experience a new message and would discover the strength hidden deep within themselves by him who loved them from the beginning and who wanted to show them that he would love them to the end.

In him is revealed to us the reality of the God in whom we believe: someone real, who, in order to meet us fully and definitively, became undividedly and unambiguously human in our concrete history, spoke our language, and shared our concerns. In Jesus of Nazareth, God tied the difficult questions about transcendence and ultimate meaning to the daily life of men and women who wonder about their bread, their love, their roof, and their dependence; about their pain, their joys, and their faults; about the future of their children and their own future; about the loss of loved ones and about individual responsibility; about what is right and what is not, what we owe and what is owed to us, what we await and what awaits us.

Thus, it is impossible to occupy ourselves with the "things of heaven" without being immediately sent back to the "things of the earth." When Vatican II affirmed that "the joys and the hopes, the griefs and the anxieties of the men of this age, especially those who are poor or in any way afflicted, these are the joys and hopes, the griefs and anxieties of the followers of Christ. Indeed, nothing genuinely human fails to raise an echo in their hearts" (*Gaudium et spes,* 1), it was only extending Saint John's meditation on the commandment (and the gift, as Benedict XVI highlighted for us) of love: "Those who say, 'I love God,' and hate their brothers and sisters are liars: for those who do not love a brother or sister whom they have seen cannot love God whom they have not seen" (1 John 4:20).

For this reason I come before you year after year to share these reflections about the "things of the earth" that are fully visible in anticipation of the "things of heaven." Because the work to which you are dedicated doubtless builds the earthly city by educating men and women, citizens of this country, members of society, scholars, artists, and workers in various spheres of human endeavor. And you are living this mission as the concrete way to advance the Christian vocation to renew the world with the power of the Gospel; and, by building the earthly city, you are also sowing the seeds of the heavenly Jerusalem, as collaborators in God's definitive work.

This mysterious interlocking of the earthly and the heavenly is the foundation for the presence of the Church in the field of education, beyond any humanitarian or altruistic impulse. This is precisely the ultimate meaning of the Church's educational mission, and the motivation for these messages that I prepare for you every year.

Once again I invite you to reflect on your responsibility as educators for building the earthly city. This year I specifically want to focus on the challenge of forming persons as responsible, supportive citizens, with a historical and collective sense of the community, from the roots of their identity and their self-consciousness of the common destiny of their people.

Why choose this theme? There are two reasons. First is its inescapable centrality in the work of the teacher. The function of the school includes a fundamental element of socialization: the creation of the social bond that turns every person into a community, a nation, and a people as well. The school's task is not exhausted by the transmission of knowledge or even in the education of values; rather, these dimensions are intimately linked to what I first stressed: the people are not a mass of subjects or consumers, or clients or citizen vote suppliers. The second reason that impels me to make this question the theme for reflection this year is precisely the need to strengthen and reestablish the social bond. In these times of globalization, postmodernity and neoliberalism, the ties that shape our nations are tending to loosen and sometimes even unravel, resulting in individualistic practices and mentalities and the "save yourself if you can" attitude that reduce social life to nothing more than a pragmatic and selfish give-and-take. This has serious consequences: mitigating the effects becomes more complicated, violent, and painful. This fuels a vicious cycle in which the degradation of the social bond creates more anomie, indifference, and isolation.

What Is It to Be a People?

By initiating this reflection on the social bond, its crisis, and the ways to strengthen it, what comes to us from the crossroads is a word that runs through the history of our country from one side to the other: the people.

"People" is more than a logical category: it is a mystical category. In 1810, people poured into the city's main square demanding "to know what this is," as we learned from the old textbooks: a group of active neighbors took park in public life during a municipal crisis. The crowd held massive demonstrations in the plazas and avenues throughout the twentieth century, with the slogan: "If this isn't the people, where are they?" Militant political and social groups, marching with the conviction that "a people united will never be defeated."

That is to say, "people" is more than a concept. It is a word charged with meaning, emotion, sewn with the history of struggle, hope, life, death, and even betrayal. Such a contradictory and controversial word! In this time of "the death of ideology," postmodernity, and the "light" attitude toward life, it has been kept high up in the closet, between grandma's things and the photos that are painful to look at, but that no one dares to take down.

Let us not forget that there once resounded strongly among us the shout "Let them go." The only thing not heard in those nights of bonfires, great nervousness, and uncertainty were voices raised to say, "Here I am, I'm committed," at least, not in sufficient quantity and vigor.

The issue of the "people" is precisely what this is about. If we were able (and we cannot and should not always) to abstract the appeal of "people" from the diverse and often antagonistic contexts in which the word was used and succeeded in mobilizing involvement in our national history, I believe that we would arrive at recognizing a fundamental meaning: the "people" can be named only from involvement, from participation. It is a word that has so much emotional burden and such projection of hopes and dreams that it becomes unnatural if it is taken only as an "objective" issue, external to what is included in its discourse. More than a word, it is a call, a con-vocation to leave the individualistic enclosure, the narrow self-interest, the little pond to enter fully into the wide flowing river that unites in itself the life and history of the broad land that it crosses and to which it gives life.

That's also why it is so feared and criticized: for the summoning strength that frees for good or for ill, in pursuit of collective causes, that either make history or illusions that culminate in scandal and pain. Why do we not shake with passion or indignation, as the case may be, given the resonance this word creates?

Dear educators, I invite you to keep delving more deeply into the meaning of the word "people" as a call to presence, participation, and committed action, to rediscover the meaning of the "people" against the background of a slogan that gives direction to our search: "Here I am. I am committed." And with the conviction that today, more than ever, we need to be a people and to dare to educate. When educational structures are being surpassed by faceless powers that circulate proposals, messages, models, and consumption with no responsibility for the consequences that they produce in young children and teenagers, we have to dig in our heels so we can enter deeply into the meaning of the word "people." Let us think about two directions: (1) a geography and a history; (2) a decision and a destiny.

A Geography and a History
First, a people is tied to geography, or rather, to a land. It is sometimes said that there are plains people, mountain people, and other environmental specifications that, without losing meaning, are easily outstripped by the dynamics of modern, predominantly urban societies that are characterized by all manner of crossbreeding, intertwining, and mutations. Nonetheless, geography has a force of attraction as a landscape not so much "touristic" as existential and also as a matrix of symbolic references that, upon being shared, create collective meanings and values.

Perhaps we should re-read this dimension in the center of the big city and think of the neighborhood as the site of roots and everyday life. The growth of the city and the rhythm of life has largely made the neighborhood lose the gravitational pull it once had, but many of its elements are still a force, even in the whirlwind of fragmentation. This is because the neighborhood (or the land), as a common space, involves a variety of colors, flavors, images, memories, and sounds that make up the framework of daily life, of that which, precisely because it is small and imperceptible, is essential. The people of the neighborhood, the colors of the football club, the plaza with its transformations and histories of games, love, and companionship that happened there, the street corners and meeting places, the memory of grandparents, the sounds of the street, the music and texture of the light on that block, this corner—all this powerfully creates the feeling of identity. Personal and shared identity, or, rather, personal as much as shared.

Will the logic of unchecked market growth turn all spaces into something merely functional? And will this condemn the dimension of roots to death? In a short time, will we travel only through virtual or virtualized spaces by means of screens and freeways? Or will it be better if we find new ways to plant symbols in our surroundings, to define space, to live?

To be a people means to inhabit a space together. Here we have, then, a first path by which to relaunch our response to the call: to open our eyes at what and at whom surround us in the sphere of daily life; to restore the neighborhood, the care, the welcome; to break the siege of mortal selfishness recognizing that we live next to and with others who are worthy of our attention, friendship, and affection. There is no social bond without this first, almost microscopic, daily dimension: being together in the neighborhood, exchanging a few words at different times of the day, worrying about what affects all of us, helping each other in the small things of everyday life.

And this is a special point of reflection for us: the neighborhood school actively contributing to making connections, creating identity, valuing shared space. The school that links families in it and with the larger community of the neighborhood, with its institutions and the networks that shape the life of the city. The school is the reference point and heart of the neighborhood for so many families, provided it is well integrated in its reality and not an island attending only to its internal challenges.

The spatial dimension, in addition, is linked with another, just as fundamental, if not more so: that of time become history. People spent their childhood in the neighborhood where their sons and daughters are living now and will remember tomorrow. The homeland also evokes that fragment of space where parents are buried. And what unites us in the shared space, beyond immediate practical issues, is the legacy of those who lived before us and the responsibility we have for those who follow. Legacy and responsibility that materialize in shared values and symbols.

A people, then, is a historical reality constituted through many generations. And for this reason it has the capacity to continue to exist beyond crises. But, in addition, human time passes with the transmission from one generation to the next. Generational transmission always has something of continuity and of discontinuity. The child is similar to the parent but distinct. A child is not a clone: there is something that continues from one generation to the next, but there is also something new, something that changed. A people is necessarily dynamic. The culture of a people, the common values and symbols that identify them, is not the sclerotic repetition of the same, but rather vital creativity on the base of what was received. That's why culture is never uniform; rather, by changing in multiple levels and lines, it includes diversity. Only expressions that try to "fix" or "freeze" the life of the people end up being exclusionary. A living culture has a tendency to openness, integration, multiplication, sharing dialogue, giving and receiving in the very heart of the people and with other people with whom relations develop.

The reconstruction of the social bond, the response to the call to be a people, the getting involved in doing something for the common good, implies an attentive listening to the legacy of those who came before us and an openness to the new meanings that those coming after us will create or propose. In other words, an engagement with history. There is no viable society contracted in time to the pure present. To be a people demands a long, wide look in order to include all those that it can and to constitute its own identity in creative fidelity to what was and continues to be, though renewed, and to what is not yet but is announced in various ways in a present rooted in what has been.

Why not consider our schools as privileged places of dialogue between generations? We are not talking only of "having parent meetings" to get them involved in our work as teachers or to contribute to the resolution or containment of their children's problems, but also to think of new ways to foster the awareness of a common history, the perception of its meaning and the appropriation of values amassed in it. It's also about finding a way to interest young children and teenagers in the concerns and desires that their elders (and the elders of the elders) left as unfinished work, and to provide them with the resources needed for the creative (and even critical, if it is necessary) pursuit of those dreams.

A Decision and a Destiny

However, the historical dimension of the meaning of people does not refer only to the way in which the past is understood and taken on in the present but also to openness to the future through a commitment to a common destiny. It's about the assertion, proclaimed so many times and lived with even more difficulty, that "no one is saved alone." To think of realization and transcendence as an endeavor of the whole collectivity, and never outside of it, is what permits turning the "many" (and distinct) into a community. Human diversity lived as division and differences understood as hostility are a fact of the experience of real history.

No special divine revelation is needed to make us realize that humankind is marked by every kind of division; it manifests itself in mutual mistrust, battles for supremacy over one another, wars and exterminations, deceptions and lies of all kinds. How much more in a country like ours, which since its birth has been marked by a mixtures of races, cultures, and religions, with the burden of ambiguity ("light and shadow") that human history carries!

But, on the other hand, to be a people does not mean to be overwhelmed (its own subjectivity, desires, freedom, and awareness) by a sought-after "totality" that would really not be anything more than an imposition by some on the rest. The "common" of community can only be "for all" the people if it is at the same time "for each one" of us. Symbolically we can say that there is no "single language" but the unique capacity to understand one another in our own language, as happened at Pentecost (Acts 2:1–11).

What unites us, what allows us to break the armor of selfishness in order to recognize ourselves in the present and build up retrospectively our past history, is the origin and also the possibility of a common future. And this possibility is what starts the creation of the mediations necessary for this future to begin being built now in the present: institutions, evaluation criteria, productions (e.g., scholarly and artistic) that focus on the meaning of the lived and the hoped for, serving as a beacon in the ambiguous center of human time. All of this demands an attitude similar to that of the sower: to plan for the long term without ceasing to act always at the right moment and, above all, in the today; a way of thinking, a way of assessing situations, a way of leading and educating, a way of acting in the here and now without losing sight of the sought-after horizon.

To build up the social bond we need to think not only in "the medium and long term" but also to think "big." The best future we can dream of must be the measure and the lens that determines the direction of our actions and the quality of our contribution. "Broad" (for all and with all) and "effective" (striving to create the systems and necessary mediations to move toward those goals). We are speaking of mediations that are political (of which the state is the most important, no matter what the concrete form may be), legal, social, educational and cultural, without excluding the religious, whose contributions go far beyond the simple circle of believers.

I will return to these issues later in more detail. For now, I want to leave you with one last idea by way of conclusion.

In our efforts to discover the dimensions that give life to a community and strengthen the social bond, let us call to mind Saint Augustine's definition: "a people is an assemblage of rational people held together by a common agreement as to the objects of their love." This "common agreement" is shaped, as we have already noted, in common actions (values, fundamental attitudes toward life, symbols) that generation after generation take on a special profile unique to this community.

But to speak of "common agreement" or of "common destiny" implies, in addition to a series of habits, a determination to walk in this direction, without which everything else is hopeless. This implies a humble, contemplative openness to the mystery of the other, which becomes respect, the full acceptance that begins not with "tolerant indifference" but with the committed practice of a love that affirms and fosters the freedom of every human being and enables us to build together a lasting, living bond.

In this way we can locate the question of "being a people" in the root that essentially constitutes it, at least from our perspective: love as the deepest reality of the social bond. This will enable us to continue our reflection by a course I consider indisputable.

Who Is My Neighbor?

I want to clarify something: this message is not intended to be a philosophical grounding for the social bond in new times. Others can do it and are doing it, without doubt much better than I. Rather, what I want to do is invite you to think about basic roots and what it is that we have lost in the change of epochs. Why haven't the great advances of the last few decades made us happier as a people? In this way, perhaps we can describe the "clues" that allow us to contribute our grain of sand (as teachers, parents, citizens) for the alternative construction, using the beautiful expression of Pope Paul VI: "for the building up of a civilization of love."

Permit me to suggest a couple of clues that I find in the Gospel.

The first revolves around a teaching of Jesus that I dare to call fundamental: the parable of the Good Samaritan (Luke 10:25–37). I have already commented on this text on other occasions, but it seems to me that it can never be emphasized enough. Because the only way to rebuild the social bond to live in friendship and peace is to start recognizing the other as a neighbor, that is, for us to become neighbors. What does this mean? A basic ethical framework, which gives us such invaluable ideas as "human rights," proposes treating the human person always as an end, never as a means. That is to say, I do not value and acknowledge the other for what he can give me or for how he can serve me. Nor for his social utility or economic productivity. All of this is treating him as a means for something else. To consider him always as an end is to recognize that everyone is human, and for this reason alone he is my fellow human being, my neighbor. Not my competitor, my enemy, my potential aggressor. This acknowledgment should be given as a principle, as a fundamental position toward any human being, and also in practice as behavior and activity.

However, why am I going to consider this person, of whom I know nothing, who has nothing to do with me, as my neighbor? How is he neighbor to me? What does it bring me to become his neighbor? The parable of the Good Samaritan adds to the modern formulation a dimension without which, in my opinion, runs the risk of becoming an abstract imperative, a formal call to self-sustaining responsibility: internal motivation.

Why did the Good Samaritan put the injured man on his shoulder and ensure that he received the care and attention that the others, more schooled in the Law and the commandments, had denied him? In the Gospel, the parable appears as an explanation of the teaching about love of God and of neighbor in the two fundamental and inseparable dimensions of the Law. And if the Law, far from being a simple external obligation or the fruit of a pragmatic "negotiation," was that which constituted the believer as such and as a member of a community, that foundational bond with God and his people outside of which the Israelite could not even think of himself, then to love our neighbor by becoming a neighbor is what constitutes us as human beings, as persons. To recognize the other as neighbor "brings" me nothing in particular: it constitutes me as a human person; and so, it is the foundation on which a human community, not a horde of wild animals, is constituted.

The Good Samaritan put his neighbor on his animal because only in this way could he consider himself a "neighbor," a somebody, a human being, a child of God. Notice how Jesus inverts the reasoning: it is not a question of recognizing the other as a neighbor but of recognizing ourselves as capable of being neighbors.

What else is sin, in this context of relations between persons, but the fact of refusing to "be neighbor"? In this way, the idea of sin is taken out of the legalistic context of "not doing any forbidden things" and put into the very center of the freedom of the person placed face to face with the other. A freedom called to inscribe itself in the divine meaning of things, creation, and history, but also tragically capable of being transformed into some other possible meaning that always ends in suffering, destruction, and death.

The first "clue" then: to believe that everyone is my brother or sister, to become a neighbor, is the condition of possibility of my own humanity. From that, the whole task for which I am responsible (and I stress whole task) is to look for, invent, test, and improve concrete ways of living this reality. The teaching vocation is a privileged space to put this into practice. Every day, every morning, you have to invent new ways to acknowledge—to love—your students and to foster mutual recognition—their love for one another. To be a "teacher" is thus, above all, a way to "exercise humanity." A teacher is one who loves and teaches the difficult task of loving every day, by personal example of course but also by helping to create devices, strategies, and practices that help to make this basic truth a possible and effective reality. Because to love is a great deal more than feeling affection and emotion once in a while. It is completely a challenge to creativity. Once again it is to invert the usual reasoning. First, it is a question of becoming a neighbor, of telling ourselves that the other is always worthy of our love. And it remains to be seen how, by what paths, and with what energy. It is to find the way (surely different every time) to examine the failings, limitations, and even wrongdoings (in your case, of students), to be able develop a love that is, concretely, acceptance, recognition, promotion, service, and gift.

Perhaps it can be a morning exercise (and also a self-examination before sleeping): What am I going to do today in order to effectively love my students, my family members, my neighbors? What "tricks" am I going to use to confuse and overcome my selfishness? What support will I seek for myself? What ground am I going to prepare in the other, in the groups I am part of and in my own conscience; what seeds am I going to plant so I can finally love my neighbor; and what fruits do I foresee picking today? Thus, becoming neighbors is a loving undertaking. In this way we are human beings: always working to become what we are from the beginning.

When Was It That We Saw You Hungry and Gave You Food?

The second "clue" is another teaching of Jesus about love: the parable of the Final Judgment (Matthew 25:31–46). The Good Samaritan showed us that personal love, face to face, is absolutely essential so that we humans can be effectively human, so that the community of the people can be too, and not just a aggregate of personal interests. But, it would be more precise to indicate its limits and the need to give shape to love's "long arms." Because though in the immediacy of the face to face is love's great strength, it is not enough. Let's take a look.

The immediacy of the "face to face" can prevent us from seeing what is important. It can be exhausted in the here and now. By contrast, a truly effective love, a deep-rooted solidarity, as I said to you in my message of last year, has to work out reflexively the relationship between clearly painful and unjust situations and the discourses and practices that give birth to and reproduce them, with a view to adding to the hugs, personal support, and companionship some effective solutions that could put a stop to the suffering, or, at least, reduce it.

On the other hand, love understood only as the immediacy of the response in the presence of my neighbor's face can be affected by another weakness, quite characteristic of the sinners that we are: to immediately become conduits for our need for showmanship or for self-redemption. What impressive depth and psychological finesse do the Lord's words reveal when he speaks about giving alms: "When you give alms, do not let your left hand know what your right hand is doing" (Matthew 6:3), or when he criticizes the Pharisee who stands and prays before the altar feeling satisfied with his virtue (Matthew 18:9–14)!

The parable of the Final Judgment makes us discover other aspects of love that are at the base of all human community and social friendship. I want to call your attention to a detail in the text: those who were declared "blessed" by the Son of Man were those who had fed him and given him something to drink, had welcomed, clothed, and visited him, but without knowing that they had done this. That is to say, the direct awareness of having "touched" Christ in their brother, of having been a true neighbor of the wounded Lord at the side of the road, is given only after the fact, when "all has been accomplished." We never know everything when we are truly reaching out to persons with our actions. We will not know, sadly or happily, until these actions have produced their effects.

Obviously, this does not refer to what we can do directly as a response to the "face to face," which is fundamental, but to another dimension that is connected to this first attitude. "When did we give you something to eat, to drink, etc." is about a love that becomes effective "over time," at the end of a trajectory. Concretely, I am referring to the institutional dimension of love. The love that passes through institutions in the broadest sense of the word: historical forms that concretize intentions and desires and make them last. What, for example? Laws, established forms of living together, social mechanisms that ensure justice, fairness, and participation—the duties or obligations of a society that at times irritate us and seem useless, but that over time make possible a life in common in which all can exercise their rights, not just those who have the power to demand them or to dominate.

The parable of the Last Judgment thus speaks to us of the value of institutions in the recognition and promotion of persons. We can say it like this: "When the Son of Man comes in his glory," he will ask us to account for all those times we did or did not do our "duties," whose consequences on the level of love we could not visualize directly; they are part of the commandment of love. We also include the duty of participating actively in "public affairs," instead of sitting back to watch or criticize.

And here it is essential to highlight again the greatness of the teaching vocation, the enormous social and even political relevance, in the deepest sense of the word, that this daily, selfless task, so little acknowledged in some quarters, has. To educate is a gesture of love. Education is a genuine expression of social love. There is a true paradox in the mission of teachers: the more attentive they are to detail, to the small things, to the singularity of each student and the contingency of each day, the more their actions are linked to the common, to the great, to what makes the people and the nation. For teachers, participation in public affairs is close to what they do every day (without giving, because of this, less value to other forms of social or political activity or involvement). On the contrary, the "work" of going to school every day and facing, without ever letting up, the challenge of teaching, educating, and socializing children and youth is a task whose social relevance will never be adequately highlighted. "Educate the sovereign!" is not just a grandiloquent slogan from the past.

Conclusion: Five Proposals to Help Re-create the Social Bond

As is becoming already a tradition in these messages, I will propose five practical ideas that, in some way, summarize and outline an operational resolution of the reflections developed. I hope they will serve to open up dialogue in the communities and give rise to new initiatives.

1. Christian Faith as a Force of Freedom

The first proposal is to recognize once again the immense capacity for renewal of the culture that the Gospel possesses. Our involvement as citizens and our task as teachers cannot be separated from an explicit faith as the active principle of meaning and action. It's true that in a society that is recently learning to live together in plurality, conflicts and various disappointments are often created. Given these difficulties, we Catholics have not a few times felt tempted to keep quiet and hide ourselves, attempting to block the chain of mutual misunderstandings and condemnations, to which so many times, by not recognizing it, we will have contributed by our errors, sins, and omissions. My proposal is this: let us dare to recover the liberating potential of the Christian faith, which is capable of animating and deepening democratic coexistence by injecting real, lived fraternity. As the Church in Argentina, we who are baptized are not lacking in sins of which we are ashamed and for which we repent, but neither do we lack for examples of dedicated witnesses committed to peace and justice, to the authentic Gospel radicalism of service to the poor, and to the pursuit of a free, inclusive society and a life more worthy of our people. Let us recover the memory of so many Christians who have given their time, their ability, and even their lives throughout our nation's history. They are a living testimony that a faith assumed, lived deeply, and confessed publicly is not only not incompatible with the aspirations of contemporary society but can, in fact, bring to it the humanizing power that at times seems to be diluted in postmodern culture. In every one of our schools may the memory of so many of our brothers and sisters who gave the best they had to build up a homeland of justice, freedom, and fraternity be transmitted and honored, and may it be actively sought in every one of our institutions to create new forms of witness to a living and life-giving faith!

2. All Voices, Every One

The reconstruction of a truly inclusive and democratic social bond demands of us a renewed practice of listening, openness, dialogue, and even coexistence with other tendencies without thus failing to prioritize the universal and concrete love that should always distinguish our communities. Concretely I am proposing that as Christian teachers you open your mind and your heart to the diversity that is increasingly a feature of the societies of this new century. While we see that all manner of fundamentalist intolerance is taking hold of relations between persons, groups, and peoples, let us live and teach the value of respect, the love beyond all differences, the value of the priority of the condition of all human beings as children of God above whatever their ideas, feelings, practices, and even their sins may be. While in today's society there is a proliferation of ghettos, closed-minded logic, and social and cultural fragmentation, let us take the first step so that all voices may resound in our schools. Let us not be resigned to enclosing ourselves in a fragment of reality. To acknowledge, accept, and live together with all ways of thinking and being does not imply rejecting your own beliefs.

Accepting diversity from our own identity means giving testimony to who we are without "eliminating" the other. Let us struggle, in the classroom and in all those places we find ourselves as teachers, against the practice of excluding others a priori for social, economic, political, religious, cultural, or personal reasons. May there be no place for intolerance and exclusion in our hearts, our words, our schools, or our classrooms.

3. Reevaluate Our Cultural Productions

The momentum of plurality, of diversity, does not exhaust the dynamic of the social bond: to be precise, it goes hand in hand with the centrifugal force of the unity of the "many and the distinct." But as our own history teaches us about the sterility of any "forced unification," we will have to support the "long road," the road of testimony to our identity through the summoning power of art and historical production. This implies a definite act of confidence in the value of our works of art, our literary productions, our many expressions of historical, political, and esthetic thought, in their authenticity and in the energy they possess to awaken the meaning and value of community.

For several years now I have proposed a "situated" reading of our national poem, the "Martín Fierro." We should proceed along this line. Argentina has provided the world with quality writers and artists (and I include those who speak of the "local" but touch on the more "universal" fiber of humankind, as the classics did). This includes the area of academics as well as of art and popular culture. Why not insist on and promote reading, listening to, and contemplating these, thereby recovering some of the space that has been taken over by so many shallow productions imposed by the market? So many novels infinitely superior to the best sellers that fill the supermarkets, so much music—of all genres, from the most traditional to those that express the view of the youngest generations—that say something of what we are and what we want to be!

What beauty is embodied in the visual arts, in architecture, so much reflection and debate with the irony and sparkle that characterize our great journalists and thinkers on the disparate circumstances of our history, so much cinema that "tells" our stories and our history!

I am not proposing to revive chauvinistic ideologies or a supposed superiority of the "national" over regional cultures. To reevaluate what is ours does not in any way mean to ignore the great richness of universal culture. Rather, it is about re-creating a sense of being a people by once again hearing and telling the stories of our people, as in a family the children have to listen at one time or another to the details of their parents' and grandparents' lives. The identity of the people (like the identity of each person) is mostly formed by storytelling, by situating events in a timeline and a horizon of meaning. It's about telling and saying again who we are, and about listening to what has been said, again finding ourselves situated before the tracks that our ancestors created through their life and work and have left for us. In this aspect it's important to bear in mind that the process of globalization can install itself in two ways. The first moves in the direction of uniformity, in which the person ends up being a point in the perfect global sphere. Here particularities are wiped out. The second way comprises an eagerness for the unity and collaboration of persons and peoples, uniting them globally but preserving the unity of each particularity. The shape is no longer a sphere but a polyhedron: unity in diversity. The second form of globalization is the acceptable one.

4. Pay Attention to the Institutional Dimension of Love

By way of finalizing, I want to insist on the importance of organized ways of participating in our common life. We Argentineans have a tendency to devalue the law, the norms for living together, and the duties and responsibilities of social life, from the old "rules of courtesy," which are virtually nonexistent nowadays, to legal obligations like the paying of taxes, among others. All this is essential so that our living together is on a firmer basis, more respectful of the person and more likely to create a sense of community. This business of "under the table," "the rascal," and "the smart alec" does not help to overcome this stage of anomie and fragmentation. It is necessary that we fully support the strengthening of the many instances of participation in, and protection of, what is shared, and what has been continually undermined by our history of arrogance, violence, arbitrariness, selfishness, and indifference.

5. Celebrate Together the Love of God

Finally, this love of being with youth, this enjoyment of feeling part of an experience that surrounds them and gives them identity, may be pointing us to a path that brings us nearer to proposing to them the value of celebrating the sacred mysteries. It's true that, in the culture of the useful and the pragmatic, worship's gratuitousness and apparent lack of utility do not seem to make it attractive; however, it is interesting that all this sensitivity to warm encounter, combined with a taste for music and its other artistic aspects, is a way of approaching the development of a culture open to God and with a capacity for deep empathy for the human, a culture that knows how to worship and pray and, at the same time, enables a strong, intense commitment to the world of men and women of today. Accordingly, we cannot allow ourselves to waver; we must take responsibility for the profound human heritage we pass on to children and youth when we lead them to the sublime act of worshiping God, both in solitude and in liturgical action.

So, we see more clearly the enormous process of conversion that the re-creation of the social bond requires. We need to re-create our institutions and to trust again in the mechanisms that, as a people, we have produced to move toward collective happiness. And this is everyone's task: rulers and ruled, strong and weak, those who have and are able and those who have little and are less able. Everyone: not just passively, accomplishing the minimum and expecting it all from others. Everyone: daring to create conditions, possibilities, and concrete strategies to bring us together again and be a people. We have experienced such a horrible history that "not being involved in anything" passes as being synonymous with integrity and virtue. Perhaps the moment has arrived (and none too soon!) to leave this mentality behind to recover the desire to be committed actors with values and truly noble causes, this mentality which is entirely cast aside in a final dialogue like this one:

"Lord, when was it that we gave you no food or drink?"

"When you added 'stay out' while I was dying of hunger, thirst, cold, thrown out into the streets, 'unschooled,' poisoned by drugs and resentment, abandoned in a society where everybody cared only for their own possessions and security."

Let us recall how the psalm expresses what we so ardently want for our land: "How very kind and pleasant it is when kindred live together in unity! . . . For there the Lord ordained his blessing, life forevermore" (Psalm 133:1, 3b). This prayer asks for Christian love to move us to create a people in which all of us can enjoy the blessedness of "having been there" when hunger, thirst, sickness, loneliness, and injustice were crying out for authentic, effective answers.

We still have time. Together with this proposal, let us reflect on the failure to which the opposite path would lead us—the dissolution and death of our country's people. Thinking about this negative countercultural phase of destruction and fragmentation, we would do well to recite with the northern poet:

> Our country died a long time ago
> in the little village.
> It was a homeland almost adolescent.
> It was hardly a little girl.
> We watched over it a little; a group
> of kids at the school.
> For most of the people
> it was a day like any other.
> We put on the white school smock
> the blackened braids.
> The Virgin of Luján and a
> round, blue rosette.
> A few wise men were opining:
> "It would be better if it died."
> "It was only a country," he told us
> the people of the village.

But we were sad. This country
was our homeland.
It's very sad to be the country's orphan.
Then we realized.
So, it's very sad
to be the country's orphans.
May we not have to say
"Later we realized."

Educating, a Shared Commitment

EASTER GIVES US the perfect opportunity to reflect on our identity, task, and mission and to share the concerns and hopes that the educational endeavor awakens in all of us. Educating is a shared commitment.

The education of children and youth constitutes a very delicate reality in what it does to their formation as free and reasonable subjects, to their formation as persons. It affirms their dignity, an inalienable gift that springs up from our original reality as image of God. And because it has to do with true human development, education is the concern and task of the Church, called to serve humankind from the heart of God and in line with a transcendent destiny that no historical condition can or will be able to overshadow.

Paschal Character of the Educational Task

The entire history of salvation shows God's merciful insistence on offering his grace to a humankind that from the beginning experienced confusion about the means and quality of its destiny. The Book of Genesis, by poetically presenting to us the first brushstrokes on this huge painting, situates the fundamental conflict of human history in the acceptance and rejection,

---

Message to the Educational Communities, 2007.

through Adam and Eve, of divine filiation and its direct implications: to live your humanity as a gift, to which you must respond by acting responsibly; and this in a climate of dialogue with and listening to the Word of God that points out the way and warns against possible or actual detours.

A similar alternative passes through human history from the Easter apex that the absolute obedience of the man on the cross and his destiny in the Resurrection achieve to each moment that our personal and collective freedom is put into play. As the whole of human history continues realizing the plan of salvation, human life moves toward its fullest perspective between the offer of grace and the seduction of sin.

Education involves the task of promoting the responsible freedom to make choices in this crossroads sensibly and intelligently; persons who understand without hesitation that their life, and that of their community, is in their hands, and that this freedom is a never-ending gift comparable only to the ineffable dimension of their transcendent destiny.

This is what is involved when you go to your schools every day and face your daily tasks—nothing more and nothing less, although at times tiredness and difficulties may instill doubts and temptations, and the effort seems insufficient, given the colossal difficulties of every kind that obstruct the path. In the face of these temptations, these stumbling blocks, there is a voice that says over and over, "Do not be afraid."

"Do not be afraid" because there is a stone that was removed once and for all: the stone that sealed the tomb of Christ, confining the faith and the hope of the disciples to a mere nostalgic memory of what could have been but was not. That stone that tried to deny the proclamation of the Kingdom that had categorically constituted the centerpiece and nucleus of the Teacher's preaching, and to reduce the newness of God-with-us to another (failed) good intention. That stone that became the priority of life over death, of the human being over the Sabbath, of love over selfishness, and of the word over mere force, in a derisory refrain proper to the weak and the deluded. This stone, destructive of hope, was removed by God himself. It was smashed to pieces once and for all.

"Do not be afraid," the angel said to the women who went to the tomb. These four words resonated in the depths of the memory; they awakened the beloved voice that so many times had urged them to leave aside all their doubts and fears; and it revived the hope that immediately became faith and over-flowing joy in the encounter with the Risen One who offered them the never-ending gift to remember everything in order to expect everything. The Lord likely repeated "Do not be afraid: I am with you always" more than once to his small group of followers, and he will keep repeating it when this small group accepts the challenge of being a light to the peoples, firstfruit of the new world. "Do not be afraid," he says to those of us who today are confronted by a task that appears to be so difficult, in a context that is reluctant about certainties and in the face of a social and cultural reality that seems to condemn all our initiatives to a kind of a priori failure, because this is nothing other than discouragement and distrust.

"Do not be afraid." Your task as Christian educators, no matter where it is carried out, participates in the newness and power of Christ's resurrection. Its paschal character takes nothing away from your task's autonomy as service to humanity and to the national and local community, but it provides it with a transcendent meaning and motivation, and a power that does not come from any pragmatic consideration but from the divine source of the call and the mission that we have decided to take on.

A Service to Humanity That Promotes Authentic Dignity

You are educators; to be an educator is to be committed to working in one of the most important ways of promoting the human person and his dignity. And to be a Christian educator is to do it from a conception of the human being that has characteristics that distinguish it from other perspectives.

Of course, it's not about division and confrontation. By dedicating part of her efforts, persons, and infrastructure to education, the Church participates in a task that benefits the whole society and should be guaranteed by the state. She does not do so to differentiate herself by proselytizing pettiness to compete with other groups or with the state itself for the "soul" and "mind" of persons, but rather to bring what she considers a treasure from the depository to share, a light that she received to make her radiant in the open. The only reason that we have anything to do in the field of education is the hope in a renewed humanity, according to God's design; it is the hope that arises from Christian wisdom, that in the risen Jesus the divine status to which we are called is revealed to us.

Let us not forget that the mystery of Christ "fully reveals man to himself," as John Paul II said in his first encyclical. There is a truth about the human person that is not the property or heritage of the Church, rather of the whole of humanity, but that the Church holds as a mission to reveal and promote. This is your territory, Christian educators. Why not be filled with pride, even more, with excitement and reverence, given the delicate and fundamental task to which you have been called?

To support your involvement in this humanizing advance, I will share with you a few thoughts about the Christian conception of the human being and his destiny.

Christian Anthropology:
An Anthropology of Transcendence

In the message for the World Day of Peace this year [2007], Benedict XVI proposed that we again consider the value and dignity of the human person. I would like to take one of the affirmations mentioned in that message and add it to this ecclesial meditation.

The pope spoke of a transcendent dignity, expressed in a kind of natural "grammar" that emerges from the divine plan of creation. This transcendent aspect is perhaps the most characteristic mark of the entire religious conception of the human being. The true measure of who we are is calculated not only in relation to the order given by natural, biological, ecological, even social factors; rather, in the mysterious bond that, without freeing us from our solidarity with the creation of which we are a part, relates us with the Creator not simply as "part" of the world but rather as its "culmination." Creation "is transcended" in the human being, the image and likeness of God: the human being is not only Adam—he is above all Christ, the first in the divine plan in whom all things were created.

And note that this gives rise, in Christianity, to a rather unique conception of transcendence—a transcendence that is not "outside" the world! To be situated fully in our transcendent dimension has nothing to do with separating ourselves from created things, with our "rising above" this world. It consists in acknowledging and experiencing the true "depth" of the created order. The mystery of the Incarnation is that which marks the dividing line between Christian transcendence and any other kind of spiritualism or gnostic transcendentalism.

Accordingly, the opposite of a transcendent conception of

the human person would be not only an "immanent" vision of him but one that is "inconsequential."* This may seem like a play on words. Something that is inconsequential is insignificant, transient, that leaves us nothing, something that we can forgo without losing anything. But let us not be confused: this play on words in itself is not inconsequential. It reveals an essential truth. When the human person loses his divine foundation, his life, his entire existence, starts to become blurred, diluted, and "inconsequential" again. What made him unique and essential falls to earth. His foundation loses everything that made his dignity something inviolable. And from here the human person, once again inconsequential, becomes one more piece in some jigsaw puzzle, a pawn on a chessboard, one more input in any type of production chain, one more number. Nothing transcendent, just one more of many components that are all inconsequential, all insignificant in themselves, all interchangeable.

We have seen, and see every day, this way of conceiving of persons as inconsequential. Children who live, get sick, and die in the streets, and no one cares. A "little head" more or less, or worse, one "lucky kid" less (as I heard, horrified, from the lips of a television newscaster). What does it matter? A little girl abducted from her home and ignominiously enslaved in prostitution rings, which are proliferating with impunity in our country. Why were our dreams shattered? It's only one more. . . . The child who is not allowed to be born, a mother to whom no one reaches out so that she can look after the life growing within her, a father for whom the bitterness of being unable to provide his children with what they need are brought to despair or indifference. What does it matter if none of this

---

* The Spanish word is *intrascendente*.

has an impact on the numbers and statistics with which we console and tranquilize ourselves?

There is no worse anthropology than an anthropology of the inconsequential for which differences are non-existent: with the same yardstick with which any object is measured a person can be measured. "Expenditures," "collateral damage," "costs" are calculated; they begin to "transcend" in decisions when the numbers swell: too many unemployed, too many dead, too many poor, too many out of school. . . . Faced with this, what happens if we realize that an anthropology of the transcendent laughs at these petty numbers and maintains, without hesitation, that every one of these small persons has an infinite dignity, that every one of them is infinitely transcendent, that whatever is done or left undone with them is done or left undone with Christ himself . . . with God himself!

With this light we can understand in a new way the Lord's comment that "no one can serve God and Money." It's not only an issue of personal ascesis or self-discipline, of one item beside another for an examination of conscience. Money is "the universal measure of all things" in the modern world. Everything has a price. The intrinsic value of each thing is standardized with a numerical sign. Do you remember several years ago when it was said that, from an economic point of view, the purchasing of tanks or caramels was all the same if the numbers were equal? Similarly, it would be the same thing to sell drugs or books if the numbers are right. If the measure of value is a number, everything is the same if the number doesn't vary. The measure of each human being is God, not Money. This is what "transcendent dignity" means. Persons cannot be "counted" and "accounted for." A reduction of the person to a common denominator (numerical or otherwise) in himself or in other things of the world is impossible.

Everyone is unique. Everyone is totally and singularly important. Everyone should be important to us. Not one single violation of the dignity of a man or a woman can be justified in the name of a thing or idea. Not one!

Does it need to be stated that taking this seriously would be the beginning of a complete revolution in the culture, the society, the economy, politics, and even religion itself? Does it need to be stated that to name some of the normally accepted practices of modern societies would no longer be justified if the transcendent dignity of the person was put ahead of any other consideration?

Transcendent Dignity: The Human Person as Part and Culmination of Creation

First, the transcendence of the human person involves a relationship with nature.

What does this mean?

We persons have a complex relationship with the world in which we live, precisely because of our double condition as children of the earth and children of God. We are part of nature; we are subject to the same physical, chemical, and biological dynamics as are other beings that share our world. Although the affirmation "we are part of the whole" is trivialized and often misunderstood, it is an element of creation's admirable balance.

The land is our home. The land is our body. We, too, are the land. Nevertheless, for modern civilization, the human person is separated from harmony with the world. Nature has ended up as a mere quarry to be dominated, to be exploited economically. And so our home, our body, something of us, is degraded. Modern civilization has within it a biodegradable dimension.

What is the reason for this? In line with what we have been thinking about, this rupture (that will doubtless cost us and is already costing us a lot of suffering, including questions about our very survival) can be understood as a destiny of "denatured transcendence," as if the transcendence of the human person in relation to nature and the world will mean separation. We place ourselves before nature, we are confronted by nature, and in it our transcendence, our humanity, is encoded. And so we were.

Transcendence in relation to nature does not mean that we can break with its dynamic on a whim. That we are free and able to investigate, understand, and modify the world in which we live does not mean that anything goes. We didn't determine its "laws," nor are we going to ignore them without serious consequences. This is also valid for the intrinsic laws that govern our own being in the world. We humans are able to raise our heads above natural determinisms, but in order to understand their richness and meaning and to free them of their flaws, not to ignore them; to reduce chance, not to ride roughshod over purposes adapted over hundreds of thousands of years. This is the function of science and technology, which they cannot perform separated from the deep currents of life. Free, but not separated from the nature that was given to us. Science and technology move in a creative dimension: from primordial ignorance, and by means of intelligence and work, they create culture. The first form of ignorance is transformed into culture. But if the laws that nature carries within itself are not respected, then human activity is destructive and produces chaos; that is to say, a second form of ignorance is born, a new chaos capable of destroying the world and humanity.

Speaking to participants at a congress two months ago the pope warned: "Not everything that is scientifically feasible is also ethically permissible. To rely blindly on technology as the only guarantee of progress, without offering at the same time an ethical code that is deeply rooted in the same reality that is being studied and developed, would equate to doing violence to human nature, with devastating consequences for all."

Precisely because we are not only "nature" in the modern sense of the term, because we are not only physics, chemistry, and biology, we can raise questions about the meaning and structure of our natural being and locate ourselves in continuity with it. That is to say, with wisdom, and not with arbitrariness, creating "cosmos" and not "chaos."

Let us think about the multiple ramifications this idea has. As educators, you will have to take on the challenge of contributing to a new ecological wisdom that understands humankind's place in the world and that respects this human being who is part of the world. The meaning of science and technology, of production and consumption, of the body and sexuality, of the means by which we participate in the creation and transformation of the world given by God, merits rigorous reflection in our communities and classrooms, reflection that does not exclude a conversion of the mind and heart by going beyond the dictatorship of consumerism, image, and irresponsibility. Furthermore, I am not referring to spectacular actions. For example, why not turn our schools into places where a review of our consumer habits is conducted? Can we not begin to imagine, along with the families of our educational communities, new and better ways of feeding ourselves, celebrating, relaxing, choosing those objects that accompany our steps in the world? Of reevaluating what is free instead of what has worth only if it costs, to reevaluate the implication of time and work shared instead of the "already done" for rapid discard? Of reevaluating the plural and diverse beauty of persons instead of yielding to the dictatorship of standardized bodies or of differences understood as grounds for discrimination?

Transcendent humanism invites us, then, to review the way in which we are part of "nature" without reducing ourselves to it. But there is more. . . .

Transcendent Dignity: The Transcendence of Love

The transcendent dignity of the person also implies transcendence of our selfishness, constitutive openness toward the other.

The Christian conception of the human person has little to do with the postmodern enthronement of the individual as the unique subject of social life. Some authors have branded as "competitive individualism" this ideology that, after "the fall of modernity's certainties," has taken hold in Western societies. Social life and its institutions would have as their only purpose the achievement of the most unlimited possible scope for the freedom of individuals.

But, as I said to you in an earlier message, freedom is not an end in itself, a black hole behind which there is nothing, but rather it is ordered to the fuller life of the person, the entire person and all men and women. Therefore, a fuller life is a happier life. All that we can imagine as being part of a "happy life" includes my fellow human beings. There is no real, true humanism if it does not include the full affirmation of love as the bond among human beings, and in the distinctive forms that this bond is achieved: interpersonal, intimate, social, political, intellectual, etc.

This statement should seem obvious. But it is not! The primordial relation of the human person with his fellow human beings has been formulated in other ways in the history of thought and of politics. Let us recall a few definitions: "man is a wolf to man"; "before any state regulation society is a war of all against all"; "profit is the principal motor of all human activity." From some of these perspectives, man (the individual human) is free, especially to appropriate the goods of the earth and thus to satisfy his wants. It goes without saying that he will consider the other (who also wants goods) as a limit to his freedom. We already know the saying: "your freedom ends where that of others begins." That is to say, "if the others were not here, you would be more free." It is the exaltation of the individual "against" the rest; the inheritance of Cain: if it is his, it is not mine; if it is mine, it can't be his.

This "negative" definition of freedom ends up being the only one possible if we start from the absolutism of the individual; this is not the case if we let ourselves consider that every human being is essentially related to his fellow humans and his community. Indeed, if it is true that speech, one of the main, distinguishing features of the person, is not born exclusively in our interior but is amassed in words that have been passed on to me and have made me what I am (the "mother tongue," mother and language); if it is true that there is no humankind without history and without community (because nobody was born alone, as ideologies of predation and competition like to jabber on about); if our speech is always a response to a voice that addressed us first (and, ultimately, to the Voice that brought us into being), what other meaning can freedom have that does not open me to the possibility of "being with others"? Freedom, from this point of view, does not "end" but rather "begins" where that of others begins. Like all spiritual goods, it is better the more it is shared.

But to live this "positive" freedom also implies, as I indicated above, a complete "revolution" of unpredictable characteristics, another way of understanding the person and the society, a way that is based not on objects to possess but on persons to encourage and love.

Because certain things happen that should provoke alarm in us; for example, what type of madness is it when an adult is able to take a five-year-old to court because he took a toy from his child while playing in the yard? (This actually happened among us a couple of years ago!) Neither more nor less than the madness in which we are all submerged, in greater or larger measure: the madness of judging our life, personal and social, by the things we do or do not possess. The logic according to which a human being is worth what he has or is able to obtain. The logic of what I can give myself (still speaking materially) or, if we want to be more cruel, what I can steal. The logic based on the idea that human life, personal and social, is not governed by the status of each and every one of us as persons, by our dignity and through our accountability (our capacity to respond to the word that brings us together) but by relations centered on inert objects, that is to say, the insignificance of the person in relation to the simple drive to seize things! Notice how, by another path, we arrive at the same idea that we started this reflection with.

This anthropology of the inconsequential finds its pretext and its breeding ground in the hyperinflation that in the last decades has been termed the "market," an insistence (in many instances, practically an absolutizing) that from a Christian point of view can clearly be called idolatry.

Let's clarify things a little. We are not demonizing the market as a certain way of organizing our exchanges and of thinking about the world of the economy. The problem is that the idea of the "market," almost from its origin, alludes to nothing else other than a great deal of people buying and selling. Anything that cannot be bought and sold is not part of it. The problem lies in the fact that not everything can be bought and sold. Some things "have no price"; for example, the goods that we call "spiritual": love, joy, compassion, truth, patience, courage, etc. And there are other things that could be bought for their utility and necessity but are not because people lack money, ability, health, etc.

This introduces a whole new series of problems, and this is not the first time I have referred to them; for example, "to be somebody" (that is to say, "to exist" in the world of the market) it is necessary "to have" things, but if I cannot have them "by fair means" (that is, by possessing something that the market considers valuable to offer), I have little choice but to accept that "I do not exist," that there is ultimately no place for me ... or to try to have them "by foul means." And as the world of the economy is not governed so much by real necessity as by what is profitable (although it may be superfluous), there will be a great many who "do not have" but will want to "keep on being." And so those who "do have" will have to redouble their attention and add more bars so that those who were excluded do not try to enter by the windows ... those of society and also of their houses. Do you know the story? Exclusion on the one hand and self-seclusion on the other are the consequences of the internal logic of economic reductionism. Will we accept that these are "the sad laurels that we obtained"? Or will we decide to shake off the dead weight of insignificance and individualism that we have been accumulating to imagine and put into practice another anthropology?

What will be the key for this other anthropology? Citizen awareness, some will say. Solidarity. The people's consciousness. Why not redirect it to the source, though it may seem weak and romantic, and call it love? For this, truly, is one of the keys of the person's transcendent dignity.

The Transcendent Dignity of the Children of God

We arrive at the ultimate dimension of human transcendence. It is not enough to recognize and experience a new ecological consciousness that rises above any deterministic reduction to the natural–biological, and a new humanistic, unified consciousness that is opposed to the fog of individualistic, economistic selfishness. We women and men who live in the land are dreaming of a new world that in its fullness we probably will not lay eyes on, but we want it, we seek it, we dream about it. A Latin American writer once said that we have two eyes: one of flesh and the other of glass. With the eye of flesh we look at what we see; with the glass eye we look at what we dream. Poor is the woman or man, poor is the people who shut down the possibility of dreaming, who are closed to utopias. For this reason, openness to hope is part of our transcendent dignity.

A few years ago I said to you that hope is not a "spiritual consolation," a distraction from the serious tasks that require our attention, but a dynamic that frees us from all determinism and from any obstacle in order to build a world of freedom and to free this history from the all-too-familiar imprisonment of selfishness, inertia, and injustice into which we tend to fall so easily. This is a purpose of openness to the future. We are told that a future is always possible. This allows us to discover that the setbacks of today are not total or definitive, thus freeing us from discouragement, nor are the successes we achieve, thus saving us from ossification and conformism. Our status as unfinished beings, always open to something more, on the move, is revealed to us. And to our believing consciousness is added the certainty of a God who puts himself in our life and helps us along the way.

This awareness of transcendence as openness is indispensable for you, dear educators. We know that to educate is to bet on the future. And the future is governed by hope.

But Christian anthropology does not remain here. This openness is not, for the believer, only a type of fuzzy uncertainty in relation to the meaning and purpose of personal and collective history. Because it is also possible and very dangerous to overcome discouragement and conformism only to fall into a kind of relativism that loses all ability to evaluate, prefer, or choose. It is not only about building without memorable guarantees and roots. It is about being able to start building in a direction that is not left to the randomness of momentary inspirations or results, to the luck of coincidence or, ultimately, to the voice that succeeds in shouting the loudest and imposing itself on the rest.

The transcendence that reveals faith to us also tells us that this story has a direction and a conclusion. The action of God that began with a Creation, whose summit is the creature that is able to respond to him as his image and likeness, with whom he enters into a relationship of love and that reached its high point in the Incarnation of the Son, must culminate in a full, universal realization of this communion. All creation must enter into this definitive communion with God initiated in the risen Christ. That is to say, we are walking toward a conclusion that is the fulfillment, positive completion of God's loving work. This conclusion is not an immediate or direct result of human action, but of a saving action of God: it is the finishing touch on the work of art that he himself initiated and in which he included us as free collaborators. The final meaning of our existence will be resolved in the personal and communal encounter with God–Love, even beyond death.

We Christians do not believe that everything is the same. We are not going just anywhere. We are not alone in the universe. And this, which at first glance seems to be so "spiritual," can also be absolutely decisive and trigger a radical turnaround in our way of living, in the projects that we imagine and try to develop, in the meanings and values that we maintain and pass on.

True, not everybody shares our beliefs about the theological meaning of human history. But that does not have to change one iota the significance that this brings to our actions. Even when many of our brothers and sisters do not profess our Creed, it remains essential that we do—essential for us and for them, although they can't see it, provided that through this journey we will be collaborating in the coming of the Kingdom for all, even for those who have been unable to recognize it in the ecclesial signs.

The certainty that God's eschatological action will usher in the Kingdom at the end of time has a direct effect on our way of living and acting in the midst of society. It prohibits any type of conformism, takes away our excuses for compromises, and leaves us with no shady or "bent" justifications. We know that there is a Judgment, and this Judgment is the triumph of justice, love, fraternity, and the dignity of every single human being, beginning with the smallest and most humiliated; then we will have no way to be distracted. We know what side we have to be on when choosing between the alternatives that are proposed: between complying with the laws or avoiding them with "native cunning"; between telling the truth or manipulating it for our convenience; between responding to the needy that we encounter in life or closing the door in their face; between seeking and occupying a place where we can do our part in the struggle for justice and the common good, depending on the possibilities and competencies of each one of us, or "loftily disappearing," constructing our own bubble; between one or other option in every intersection of daily life, we know what side we have to be on. And this, nowadays, is no small thing.

A New Humanity That Can Start in Every School

To profess a belief and to maintain a certain way of seeing the person and loving human beings is not an attitude much in vogue in these days of relativism and the fall of certainties. "The devil loves to fish in troubled waters": the fewer certainties there are, the more room there is to convince us that the only thing solid and certain is what slogans and images about consumption propose to us.

But the last thing that we should do is to dig in defensively and bitterly bemoan the state of the world. It is not valid for us to become a priori "agents of distrust" (which is not the same as holding critical thoughts but rather its stubborn version) and to congratulate one another, in our little closed world, for our doctrinal clarity and our incorruptible defense of truth—defenses that only end up serving our own satisfaction. It is something else: it is about making positive contributions. It is to proclaim, to begin to live fully in another way, by our becoming witnesses and builders of other ways to be human beings, which is not going to happen with sullen looks and a judgmental demeanor. It is to apply our deepest vocation, not burying the denarius, but going out convinced not only that things can change but that they must change and that we can change them.

Jonah is a biblical figure who can inspire us in changing, uncertain times; he is a person who can mirror the attitudes of us who, in many cases, are educators with accumulated experience, styles, and refined ways of proceeding. He lived a tranquil, ordered life, with very clear ideas about good and bad, about how God acts and what it is that He wants at any moment, about who was faithful to the covenant and who was not. So much order led him to rigidly define the places where he had to carry out his mission to prophesy. Jonah had the recipe and the conditions to be a good prophet and to continue the prophetic tradition in the line of "what had always been done."

Suddenly, God shattered this order, bursting into his life like a torrent, taking away every kind of security and comfort to send him to the big city to proclaim what He himself would say. It was an invitation to look beyond his limits, to go to the periphery. He sent him to Nineveh, the "big city," the symbol of all the separated, alienated, and lost. Jonah was being entrusted with the mission to remind all these people, so lost, that the arms of God are open and waiting for them to return to be healed by his pardon and nourished with his love. But Jonah was unable to comprehend entirely what was being asked of him, and he fled. God was sending him to Nineveh, but he was going in the opposite direction, to Tarsus near Spain.

Fleeing is never good. The rushing makes us inattentive and we run into obstacles. Embarking for Tarsus, a storm came up, and the sailors threw him overboard because he confessed that it was his fault. When he was in the water a fish swallowed him. Jonah, who had always been so clear, dependable, and ordered, had not taken into account that the God of the covenant does not take back what he has sworn, and is "relentlessly" insistent when it comes to the good of his children. That is why, when our patience is running out, He begins to wait, making his loving word as Father gently resonate.

Just like Jonah, we can hear a persistent call that keeps inviting us to embark on this adventure to Nineveh, to accept the risk to be in the forefront of a new education, fruit of an encounter with God who is always newness and who pushes us to break out, to leave, to get moving, to go beyond the known to the periphery and the frontier where the most wounded people are and where youth, under the appearance of superficiality and conformism, keep looking for the answers to the meaning of life. In helping our brothers and sisters to find answers, we too will find renewed meaning for our actions and the taste for our vocation, the place of our prayer and the value of our commitment.

I would like to end my message, as in other years, with a few proposals that, along with others that may have occurred to you, may help to advance these wishes and objectives. I will present them as questions.

Why do we not try to live and pass on the priority of non-quantifiable values: friendship (so dear, this time in the best sense of the word, to our teenagers!), the ability to celebrate and simply enjoy the good times (although a few ants are whispering against the cicada's violin!), sincerity, which produces peace and trust, and the confidence that encourages sincerity? Easy to say, it sounds so poetic . . . but so very demanding to live it since it so often means that we tear ourselves away from the cult of efficiency and the materialism entrenched in our most deeply ingrained beliefs, and put an end to serving and worshiping the "successful management" god.

Why don't we try out new ways of encounter among ourselves, without hidden agendas? Why don't we seek out ways that the space we use in the schools can multiply its potential, imagining ways to receive the collaboration and ideas of many, making our houses places of inclusion and encounter for families, youth, the elderly, and children. It will not be easy: it demands taking into account and resolving a multitude of practical issues. But let us resolve them no matter what, and never give up trying.

Why don't we dare to incorporate in our classes more testimonies of Christians and people of good will who have dreamed of a different humanity, without expecting a perfect match with some pre-defined standard, whatever the result? We know that these kinds of figures have an enormous power as symbols of utopia and hope, more so than as models to follow to the letter. Why don't we rejoice that humanity has produced children who enabled entire generations to hold their heads high? To remember and to celebrate, in accordance with the lifestyle, culture, and history of each community, the men and women who shined, not for their millions or for the spotlights focused on them, but for the very power of their virtue and joy, for the overflowing quality of their transcendent humanity. Clearly, we came from a history of mistrust, exclusion, mutual suspicion, disqualification. Is it not time to realize that the worst that can happen to us is not to awaken dreams and hopes that will later be ripe and sustaining, but to remain in a deadly flatness in which nothing has relevance; nothing has transcendence; to remain in the culture of triviality?

Finally, why don't we set out to look for the way in which all persons recover and do not lose that which is most proper, that which is the sign par excellence of their spirit, that which is rooted in their everyday being but transcends it to the point of situating it in a position of dialogue with its Creator? There is no need to clarify it too much: I am referring to the gift of the word, a gift that requires many things on our part: responsibility, creativity, consistency. These requirements do not excuse us from daring to take the word and above all, dear educators, to give one's word. To take and to give the word, creating space for this word on the lips of our children and young people to grow, become stronger, put down roots, and to rise; accepting this word that at times can be upsetting, questioning, sometimes even hurtful, but also creative, purifying, new. . . .

The human word takes on such relevance when it becomes a dialogue with God himself, makes us great in our smallness, makes us free in front of any power because it makes habitual our dealings with him who is most able, who develops in us a special sense that at once broadens our horizons, dazzles us, and is in love with us. This cherished possibility to pray is a right that every child, every young person, can exercise. And then, what happens if we pray, if we teach our children and young people to pray?

Let us try these and other things. We will see a new humanity that will show itself beyond the reductionisms that would diminish the size of our hope. To determine what is missing, what has been lost, is not enough; we must learn to build whatever culture does not give on its own, and to dare to embody it, although we may be feeling our way and without complete certainty. This is what should be found in our Catholic schools. Are we asking for miracles? And why not?

About the Translator

MICHAEL O'HEARN has been involved in religious and university publishing for over thirty-five years. He served as director of both the University of Ottawa Press and of Novalis Publishing at Saint Paul University, where he was also a lecturer in pastoral theology. He currently works as a translator (Spanish and French) and editor of religious and academic resources.

About the Publisher

The CROSSROAD PUBLISHING COMPANY publishes CROSSROAD and HERDER & HERDER books. We offer a 200-year global family tradition of books on spiritual living and religious thought. We promote reading as a time-tested discipline for focus and understanding. We help authors shape, clarify, write, and effectively promote their ideas. We select, edit, and distribute books. With our expertise and passion we provide wholesome spiritual nourishment for heart, mind, and soul through the written word.

Also in the Pope Francis Resource Library

Open Mind, Faithful Heart
Reflections on Following Jesus

Hardcover, 320 pages, ISBN 978-08245-19971

"The secret of Pope Francis is found in this book."
—Bishop Martínez Camino

"These deeply spiritual reflections on how we follow Jesus make the perfect holiday gift, and an ideal choice for daily spiritual reading. *Open Mind, Faithful Heart* reveals like no other book the depths of Pope Francis's deep faith, joy, and compassion. It is not just for reading. It is a path for prayer and a guide for life."
—Joseph V. Owens, S.J., translator

Much is being said and written about him. To understand Pope Francis more deeply, read what he himself has published.
This book is perhaps the best introduction to what makes the Pope the engaging pastor he is. The inspiration needed to address the urgent challenges to our world and human living today is clearly outlined in this book. The spiritual foundation for much of what Pope Francis has surprised the world with since his election, radically reframing the Catholic contribution, is found in these texts, which their author wished to gather just before expecting to retire—but then being called to Rome instead. *Open Mind, Faithful Heart* offers an irreplaceable window into the heart and soul of the Pope who is changing how the world sees the Church.

Support your local bookstore or order directly
from the publisher at www.crossroadpublishing.com

The Crossroad Publishing Company